CAMBRIDGE LIBRARY COLLECTION

Books of enduring scholarly value

British and Irish History, Seventeenth and Eighteenth Centuries

The books in this series focus on the British Isles in the early modern period, as interpreted by eighteenth- and nineteenth-century historians, and show the shift to 'scientific' historiography. Several of them are devoted exclusively to the history of Ireland, while others cover topics including economic history, foreign and colonial policy, agriculture and the industrial revolution. There are also works in political thought and social theory, which address subjects such as human rights, the role of women, and criminal justice.

The History and Design of the Foundling Hospital

Captain Coram's Foundling Hospital was opened in London in 1741 for 'the maintenance and education of exposed and deserted young children'. Hogarth was a governor of the hospital – he donated several pictures, including his portrait of Coram – as was Handel, whose famous performances of his oratorio *Messiah* were given there from 1750 to raise funds. John Brownlow (1800–73), himself a foundling, became secretary of the hospital from 1849 until his retirement. He introduced improvements to the children's education and was a staunch defender of the hospital, refuting criticisms often levelled in the nineteenth century that taking in illegitimate children simply encouraged neglect. This brief account, building on his 1847 *Memoranda, or, Chronicles of the Foundling Hospital* (also reissued in this series), covers Coram, early supporters, the institution's paintings – which formed the first public art gallery in London – and the care of the foundlings.

T0382501

Cambridge University Press has long been a pioneer in the reissuing of out-of-print titles from its own backlist, producing digital reprints of books that are still sought after by scholars and students but could not be reprinted economically using traditional technology. The Cambridge Library Collection extends this activity to a wider range of books which are still of importance to researchers and professionals, either for the source material they contain, or as landmarks in the history of their academic discipline.

Drawing from the world-renowned collections in the Cambridge University Library and other partner libraries, and guided by the advice of experts in each subject area, Cambridge University Press is using state-of-the-art scanning machines in its own Printing House to capture the content of each book selected for inclusion. The files are processed to give a consistently clear, crisp image, and the books finished to the high quality standard for which the Press is recognised around the world. The latest print-on-demand technology ensures that the books will remain available indefinitely, and that orders for single or multiple copies can quickly be supplied.

The Cambridge Library Collection brings back to life books of enduring scholarly value (including out-of-copyright works originally issued by other publishers) across a wide range of disciplines in the humanities and social sciences and in science and technology.

The History and Design of the Foundling Hospital

of the Foundling Hospital

With a Memoir of the Founder

John Brownlow

CAMBRIDGE
UNIVERSITY PRESS

CAMBRIDGE
UNIVERSITY PRESS

University Printing House, Cambridge, CB2 8BS, United Kingdom

Published in the United States of America by Cambridge University Press, New York

Cambridge University Press is part of the University of Cambridge.

It furthers the University's mission by disseminating knowledge in the pursuit of education, learning and research at the highest international levels of excellence.

www.cambridge.org
Information on this title: www.cambridge.org/9781108069434

© in this compilation Cambridge University Press 2014

This edition first published 1858
This digitally printed version 2014

ISBN 978-1-108-06943-4 Paperback

B. Nebot, pinxt.   J. W. Cook, sculp.

CAPTAIN THOMAS CORAM

THE HISTORY AND DESIGN

OF THE

FOUNDLING HOSPITAL,

WITH A

MEMOIR OF THE FOUNDER.

BY

JOHN BROWNLOW,

SECRETARY OF THE HOSPITAL.

LONDON:
PRINTED BY W. & H. S. WARR, 63, HIGH HOLBORN.

1858

CONTENTS.

DIRECTIONS TO THE BINDER.

THE HISTORY AND OBJECTS

OF THE

FOUNDLING HOSPITAL.

It is related, that when Captain Thomas Coram, the Founder of this Hospital, resided at Rotherhithe, about the year 1720, his avocations obliging him to go early into the city, and return late, he frequently saw infants exposed and deserted in the public streets; and as there was but one step in his active mind from the knowledge of an evil to a desire for remedying it, he immediately set about inquiring into the probable causes for so outrageous a departure from humanity and natural affection.

He knew, what every man who studies the human heart must know—that the motive to such a dereliction of maternal duty must be beyond the ordinary casualities of indigence. He was not long in discovering the true source of the evil. He found that it arose out of a morbid morality, then possessing the public mind, by which an unhappy female, who fell a victim to the seductions and false promises of a designing man, was left to hopeless contumely, and irretrievable disgrace. Neither she nor the offspring of her guilt appear to have been admitted within the pale of human compassion: her first false step was her final doom, without

B

even the chance, however desirous, of returning to the
road of rectitude. All the consideration which was
given to her condition, was the enactment of laws to
bring her to *punishment*, after she had been driven to
the commission of the worst of crimes: for the error
of a day, she was punished with the infamy of years;
and although her departure from the path of virtue,
so far from being the consequence of a previous vicious
disposition, might have been brought about by an
artful scheme of treachery, she was branded for ever
as a woman habitually lewd. These evils necessarily
increased the quantum of crime in society, according
to the manner in which they operated upon the
unfortunate individuals under their influence;—still
no one stepped forward to provide a remedy. The
legislature, from time to time, condemned the unhappy
wretch to capital punishment who should, in the
madness of despair, lift her arm against the child of
her guilt; but it never once considered the means by
which both parent and child might be saved from
destruction: yet, by a strange perversity, those very
laws bore on the face of them evidence of the necessity
and justice of some more Christian proceeding. In
all of them, the crime for which the punishment was
awarded, is stated to have been committed from a
desire in the mother to "*avoid her shame.*" Surely
the woman who would make so great a struggle to
preserve her reputation, as to break the natural ties
which bind parent to offspring, who is willing to forego
the endearments which are the fruits of her situation,
by either sacrificing or deserting her child, cannot,

with justice, be charged as habitually lewd!—a lewd
woman has no shame to hide—she makes a show of
her guilt, and claims, in open day, the protection which
she knows has been provided for her by the poor-laws.
But when a woman, with a sense of honour, finds
herself the unsuspecting victim of treachery, with
the witness of her disgrace hanging about her
neck, in the person of her child, left to the reproach
of the world and her own conscience, and seeing no
other means of saving her character, she becomes
delirious in her despair, and vents her fury on the
consequences of her seduction—the child of her
seducer! Hence the murder and desertion of children
became alarming evils—evils which were produced and
perpetuated "*for want*" (to use the words of Captain
Coram) "*of proper means for preventing the disgrace
and succouring the necessities of their parents.*" He
therefore proposed to erect a sanctuary, to which these
wretched mothers might fly, and there deposit the
offspring and the secret of an unhallowed intercourse,
and be thus enabled to return to that path from which
they had unguardedly strayed.

This was doubtless the object of Captain Coram.
In all his memorials to persons of distinction, soliciting
their support, he ascribes to the parent, as the motive
of her cruel conduct towards her offspring, a desire to
preserve her reputation,—to "*hide her shame;*" and in
Hogarth's design, illustrating the views of the Founder,
it will be seen that he makes him hold personal communion with the penitential mother, pouring into her
heart the oil of gladness, whilst he relieves her of the

child of her sorrow. To accomplish his purpose of founding an Hospital for the objects described, Captain Coram, with his usual zeal, endeavoured to enlist the sympathies of the humane and charitable. He soon found, however, that there were obstacles in the way. They who admitted the evil, questioned the remedy, and doubted whether it might not prove greater than the disease. He was for seventeen years combating public opinion on this head, and though he at last prevailed, it was after many contests between himself and others as to the probable issue. Can it be wondered at, therefore, that in addressing the President at the first meeting of the Governors after the charter had been granted, he should throw out a suggestion, that its success could only be secured "*provided due and proper care be taken for setting on foot so necessary an establishment.*" This, besides being dictated by his own good sense, was also forced upon him by those who aided in his scheme, and was the condition upon which they gave him their support. This "due and proper care" could only refer to the selection of the objects, and it will be seen in succeeding pages with what absence of forethought the Hospital was " set on foot," and the evil consequences which arose therefrom.

At the very outset an error was committed. Captain Coram, and those who assisted him, petitioned for two objects:—first, " to *prevent* the frequent murders of poor miserable infants at their birth;" secondly, " to *suppress* the inhuman custom of exposing new-born infants to perish in the streets." Now to accomplish these objects, the Charter incorporated an " Hospital for the maintenance and education of *exposed* and *deserted* young children," thus giving a licence to that which was contrary to law, and which the memorialists were desirous to *suppress*. It was clear, therefore, that such a charter, though beneficial as regards the rights and privileges which it gave to the Governors, as a corporation, was useless as respected the main object, namely, the admission of children,—and so it proved. In the next session of Parliament, after the charter was granted, the Governors found it necessary to frame a bill to *explain* and enlarge the powers granted to them. This bill passed into a law; and the preamble affords the explanation required, by stating that the Hospital is for infants who are *liable* to be exposed in the streets, or to be murdered by their parents. Now there are two causes which may suggest themselves to the reader, as likely to lead to the exposition or destruction of infants : namely, *inability of parents to maintain them,* or a *wanton inhumanity.* With respect to the first,— though this miserable plea has been sanctioned in countries where humanity and morality have made but little progress, yet in England it is altogether without foundation, for the wise and systematic provision which has been made for the relief of *indigence*, by the institution of poor-laws, takes from poverty the desperate alternative to which it might otherwise be exposed. As to the second cause,—*wanton inhumanity,* it may be said, that however the barbarous policy of eastern countries may render callous the human heart to the calls of parental affection,—in this country, where the mild influences of Christianity strengthen and support the natural ties which bind parent to offspring, the wanton sacrifice of infant life is happily of rare occurrence. It will then be asked, "*what* children are *liable* to be exposed and destroyed by their parents?" It is answered,—the children of those wretched mothers, before described, whose combination of mental and bodily distress admits of no *partial* relief,—no relief which the poor-law can effectually bestow. These were the objects which fell under the compassionate consideration of Captain Coram, and the non-attention of the early Governors to his cautionary suggestion, produced, as might have been expected, most lamentable consequences, and caused the Founder himself to secede from the Council Board of the Institution.

EARLY ADMISSION OF CHILDREN.

The first admission of Children took place in 1741, under the following advertisement :—

"To-morrow, at eight o'clock in the evening, this house will be opened for the reception of twenty children, under the following regulations :—

"No child exceeding the age of two months will be taken in, nor such as have the evil, leprosy, or disease, of the like nature, whereby the health of the other children may be endangered; for the discovery whereof every child is to be inspected as soon as it is brought, and the person who brings it is to come in at the outward door and ring a bell at the inward door, and not go away until the child is returned or notice given of its reception ; but no questions whatever will be asked of any person who brings a child, nor shall any servant of the house presume to endeavour to discover who such person is, on pain of being discharged.

"All persons who bring children are requested to affix on each child some particular writing, or other distinguishing mark or token, so that the children may be known hereafter if necessary."

These receptions of children took place occasionally in the same manner, and were necessarily regulated by the funds of the Hospital, which being derived from private subscriptions and legacies of benevolent individuals only, were of course limited.

As the Hospital became more generally known, it will readily be supposed that the applications for admission greatly increased, so that there were frequently one hundred women at the door when twenty children only could be received. This gave rise to the disgraceful scene of women scrambling and fighting to get to the door, that they might be of the fortunate few to reap the benefit of the Asylum.

To obviate this evil a new method was adopted, by which all women bringing children were admitted into the court-room, and there sat on benches, with strict orders not to stir from their seats. Then, as many white balls as there were children to be taken in, with five red balls for every twenty children to be received, and so in proportion for any greater or less number; and as many black balls, as with the white and red, were equal to the number of women present, were put into a bag or box, which was handed round to the women; each woman who drew a white ball was sent, with her child, to the inspecting-room, that it might undergo the usual examination. Every woman who drew a black ball was immediately turned out of the house with her infant; and every woman who drew a red ball was taken, with her child, into another room, there to remain until the examination of the children for whom white balls were drawn was ended, and if, on such examination, any of those children were rejected, for reasons stated in the public notice, ballots were taken, after a similar manner for filling up the vacancies, till the whole number was completed. This plan, it is true, prevented the disgraceful scenes described; but a charity so unguardedly dispensed as to the selection of its objects, could not but open the door to fraud and abuse of the worst description. We know that no human institution, however cautiously managed, can be *wholly* free from abuse; some daring Clodius will always be found to pollute the mysteries, let the house be ever so carefully watched. If this be true in ordinary cases, surely it must have required more than common caution in setting on foot an asylum, the opening of which, if not carefully effected, would let loose as many evils as ever issued from Pandora's box. This was evidently felt by Captain Coram himself, who, in the memorial which he presented to George the Second, as a recommendation of his design, throws out the cautionary suggestion,—that its success could only be insured, *provided due and proper care be taken for*

setting on foot so necessary an establishment." He no
sooner found, therefore, that the managers were acting
upon a principle which furnished no guarantee for
the effectual operation of the charity, namely—
receiving children without establishing any test by
which the merits of each case could be ascertained,
than he opposed their proceedings; but after repeated
admonition, finding his advice disregarded by the
majority of the Committee, he left the management
of the institution altogether in their hands.*

The system above referred to continued for a
period of fifteen years, viz.:—from 1741 to 1756,
during which, 1384 children were received, or, upon
an average, ninety-two annually.

The managers, however, looked forward all along

---

* Of the particular cause of disagreement between Captain Coram and
the managing Committee there is no record. The following extract from
the will of Anthony Allen, Esq., dated 1753, shows, however, that the
Founder was supported in his objections to their proceedings by one, at
least, of his friends :—

"And whereas, many years before the obtaining the royal charter for the
Hospital for exposed and deserted young children, I did, at the instance
of that indefatigable schemist, Captain Thomas Coram, really intend some
considerable benefaction towards carrying on so good a project, and did
encourage the concurrence of other liberal benefactors, till some of the
acting Governors and Guardians of the said Hospital went counter to our
judgments and proposal pressed upon them by the said Coram, on several
occasions, which made me withhold my hand, saving the sum of sixteen
guineas I advanced as necessity urged, from time to time, towards the
immediate subsistence of the said Mr. Coram, who had exhausted his whole
substance in soliciting that charter during about seventeen years, never
meeting any relief from the said Hospital, I now will that £200. besides
the said £16 16s. so paid, be given to the use of the said Hospital, within
two years after my decease, in lieu of all claims and pretensions the said
Hospital may make on that score."

to the time when they should be able to open their
Hospital upon the most unrestricted plan, and many
were the abortive schemes suggested for the acquirement
of wealth to enable them to do so ; but it was obvious,
that no power or means, except Parliamentary, could
be devised for effectually meeting the object.   To
Parliament, therefore, the Governors appealed, having
previously ascertained that George the Second had a
good feeling towards their design.   The following
resolutions of the House of Commons, of the 6th
April, 1756, sufficiently prove the success with which
the application was attended :—

"That the enabling the Hospital for the maintenance
and education of exposed and deserted young children
to receive all the children that shall be offered, is the
only method to render that charitable institution of
lasting and general utility.

"That to render the said Hospital of lasting and
general utility, the assistance of Parliament is
necessary.

"That to render the said Hospital of general utility
and effect, it should be enabled to appoint proper
places in all counties, ridings, or divisions of this
kingdom, for the reception of all exposed and deserted
young children."

Added to these resolutions, a guarantee was given
by Parliament that it would provide the means, by
liberal grants of money, to enable the Governors to
carry out this extensive scheme of charity.

A basket was accordingly hung outside of the
gates of the Hospital, and an advertisement publicly

announced, that all children under the age of two months, tendered for admission, would be received.

In pursuance of which, on the 2nd June, 1756, being the first day of general reception, 117 children were given up to the fostering care of the state!

Though the Governors of the charity, in anticipation of parochial interference, had armed themselves with the special power of the law for their protection, yet they discovered that no authority, however great, could prevent parish officers from emptying their workhouses of the infant poor, and transferring them to this general sanctuary provided by government. Had they stopped here, the morality of their conduct would not, perhaps, have been questioned; but it was the frequent practice of these daring authorities, sometimes in conjunction with the brutal father, to rob the poor mother of her new-born infant, whilst she was in a state of helplessness from the effects of her recent confinement, and to convey it to the Hospital, that they might be rid of the burden of maintaining it. The scenes which daily occurred at the asylum from this circumstance, would have moved the stoutest heart.

The managers did all they could to prevent this infamous practice, by prosecuting the delinquents, but the motive was too strong to be put down; it continued in spite of their efforts.

When a Foundling Hospital was established in Paris, in the year 1640, its objects were limited to the children found exposed in that city, and its suburbs; and it was understood by those who furthered a similar design in this country, that its operation would, in the same manner, be confined to London and its environs. But benefits so tempting being irresistable to persons in country towns, they were determined to share with the good people of London, a privilege which they considered common to all. "There is set up in our Corporation" (writes a correspondent from a town three hundred miles distant, in one of the chronicles of the day), "a new and uncommon trade, namely, the conveying children to the Foundling Hospital. The person employed in this trade is a woman of notoriously bad character. She undertakes the carrying of these children at so much per head. She has, I am told, made one trip already; and is now set upon her journey with two of her daughters, each with a child on her back." The writer then very properly suggests, that it ought to be ascertained "whether or not these poor infants do really arrive at their destination, or what becomes of them." That such an inquiry was necessary, there is no doubt;—the sequel will prove it.

At Monmouth, a person was tried for the murder of his child, which was found drowned with a stone about its neck! when the prisoner proved that he delivered it to a travelling tinker, who received a guinea from him to carry it to the Hospital. Nay, it was publicly asserted in the House of Commons, that one man who had the charge of five infants in baskets, happened in his journey to get intoxicated, and lay all night asleep on a common; and in the morning he found three of the five children he had in charge actually dead! Also, that of eight infants brought out of the country at one time in a waggon, seven died before it reached London: the surviving child owing its life to the solicitude of its mother; who rather than commit it alone to the carrier, followed the waggon on foot, occasionally affording her infant the nourishment it required.

It was further stated, that a man on horseback, going to London with luggage in two panniers, was overtaken at Highgate, and being asked what he had in his panniers, answered, "I have two children in each: I brought them from Yorkshire for the Foundling Hospital, and used to have eight guineas a trip; but lately another man has set up against me, which has lowered my price."

This practice of transporting children from remote towns was condemned by a distinct resolution of the House of Commons, and a Bill was ordered to be brought in to prevent it; but this Bill was never presented, so that parish officers and others still continued to carry on their illicit trade, by delivering children to vagrants, who, for a small sum of money, undertook the task of conveying them to the Hospital, although they were in no condition to take care of them, whereby numbers perished for want, or were otherwise destroyed; and even in cases where children were really left at the Hospital, the barbarous wretches who had the conveying of them, not content with the gratuity they received, stript the poor infants of their clothing into the bargain, leaving them naked in the basket at the Hospital gate.*

---

* The following is a strong instance of the vicissitudes of life:—Some years

A system so void of all order and discretion, must necessarily have occasioned many difficulties : for instance, it frequently happened, that persons who sent their children to the Hospital, having nothing to prove their reception, were suspected, or, if not suspected, were charged by their malevolent neighbours with destroying them, and were consequently cited before a magistrate of the district to shew to the contrary. This they could only do by procuring an examination of the Hospital registers ; and the Governors were frequently called upon for certificates of the fact, before the party could be released. This inconvenience was, however, afterwards obviated, by the practice of giving a billet to each person who brought a child, acknowledging its reception.

But the difficulty which presented itself paramount to all others, related to the manner in which so great a number of children was to be reared. In the first year of this indiscriminate admission, the number received was 3,296 ; in the second year, 4,085 ; in the third, 4,229 ; and during less than ten months of the fourth year (after which the system of indiscriminate reception was abolished), 3,324. Thus, in this short period, no less than 14,934 infants were cast on the compassionate protection of the public ! It necessarily became a question how the lives of this army of infants could be best preserved ; and the Governors, not being able to

---

since, an aged Banker in the north of England, received into the Hospital at the above period, was desirous of becoming acquainted with his origin, when, all the information afforded by the books of the establishment was, that he was put into the basket at the gate *naked*.

settle this point among themselves, addressed certain queries to the College of Physicians, which were promptly answered, by recommending a course of treatment consonant to nature and common sense ! Children, deprived as these were of their natural aliment, required more than usual watchfulness ; and although, on a small scale, the providing a number of healthy wet-nurses, as substitutes for the mothers of infants would have been an easy task, yet, when they arrived in numbers so considerable, the Governors found that the object they had in view must necessarily fail from its very magnitude.

It has been truly said, that the frail tenure by which an infant holds its life, will not allow of a remitted attention even for a few hours: who, therefore, will be surprised, after hearing under what circumstances most of these poor children were left at the Hospital gate, that, instead of being a protection to the living, the institution became, as it were, a charnel-house for the dead ! It is a notorious fact, that many of the infants received at the gate, did not live to be carried into the wards of the building ; and from the impossibility of procuring a sufficient number of proper nurses, the emaciated and diseased state in which many of these children were brought to the Hospital, and the malconduct of some of those to whose care they were committed (notwithstanding these nurses were under the super-intendence of certain ladies—sisters of charity), the deaths amongst them were so frequent, that of the 14,934 received, only 4,400 lived to be apprenticed

out, being a mortality of more than seventy per cent !
Thus was the institution (conducted on a plan so wild
and chimerical, and so widely differing from its original
design), found to be diseased in its very vitals. The
avowed object of saving life was frustrated by a variety
of contingent circumstances; and the permanent and
two-fold benefit of which it was intended to have been
the instrument, under the regulations contemplated by
the Founder, was set aside by a system of fraud and
abuse, which entailed on the public an immense
annual expenditure,* without even *one* good result. To
establish a market for *vice* to carry on her profligate
trade without let or hindrance ; to arrest the first
step towards repentance of one yet in the infancy of
crime, by pointing out the way in which she might
perpetuate her guilt with impunity ; to break the
beautiful chain of the affections which characterizes
mankind as social beings, by giving a general license to
parents to desert their offspring, upon the barbarous
plea that they cannot easily maintain them ; to
wink as it were, at fraud, by showing how designing
persons might dispose of children entrusted to their

---

* The total expense was about £500,000 ! Several propositions were made,
for ridding the country of the burthen, and amongst them the following.—"His
Majesty having recommended the case of the Foundling Hospital to the House
of Commons, which cheerfully granted £40,000. for the support of that charity,
the growing annual expense of it appeared worthy of further consideration, and
leave was granted to bring in a bill for obliging all the parishes of England and
Wales to keep registers of all their deaths, births, and marriages, that from
these a fund might be raised towards the support of the said Hospital. The
bill was accordingly prepared by a committee appointed for the purpose, but
before the House could take the report into consideration, the Parliament
was prorogued."—*Smollett.*

guardianship, and prevent a discovery of their guilty acts : these were some of the evils which were realized in the early proceedings of the Governors, for want of attention to the cautionary suggestion of the Founder, to "take due and proper care in setting on foot so necessary an establishment."

But the state of things described could not possibly last long, except in a community lost to all decency and order. No sooner, therefore, did those who had promoted a system fraught with so much mischief, discover the error they had committed, than they wished to retrace their steps :—the moralist enlisted his pen in a cause which he found was endangered by its continuance ; and mercy stepped forward to arrest the destroying hand of death, to whose vengeance so many infants had been doomed, under the sanction of this unwise administration of the charity; and at length, Parliament, which, by its inadvertence had promoted the evil, annulled its sanction thereto, by declaring—*That the indiscriminate admission of all children under a certain age in the Hospital, had been attended with many evil consequences, and that it be discontinued.*

After the House of Commons had passed the resolution which annulled the practice of receiving children in such an unguarded and indiscriminate manner, the Governors were left to adopt what they conceived to be the views of the Founder, and to place the institution upon that basis of prudential charity on which it now stands.

Tokens.—It will be seen, that one of the regulations at the outset was, that persons leaving children should "affix on them some particular writing, or other distinguishing mark or token." Fifty years ago, the Governors being curiously inclined, appointed a committee to inspect these tokens, with the view of ascertaining their general nature, which committee, having examined a portion of them, reported the following to be specimens of the whole : viz.—

A half-crown, of the reign of Queen Anne, with hair.

An old silk purse.

A silver fourpence, and an ivory fish.

A stone cross, set in silver.

A shilling, of the reign of James the Second.

A silver fourpence, of William and Mary, and a silver penny of King James.

A silver fourpence.

A small gold locket.

A silver coin (foreign), of sixpence value.

In 1757, a lottery ticket was given in with a child, but whether it turned up a prize or a blank is not recorded.

The following lines were pinned to the clothes of one of the deserted infants :—

> " Go, gentle babe, thy future life be spent
> In virtuous purity, and calm content;
> Life's sunshine bless thee, and no anxious care
> Sit on thy brow, and draw the falling tear;
> Thy country's grateful servant may'st thou prove
> And all thy life be happiness and love."

Another child, received on the first day of admission, had the following doggrel lines affixed to its clothes :—

"Pray use me well, and you shall find
My father will not prove unkind
Unto that nurse who's my protector,
Because he is a benefactor."

At this period, the station in life of the parties availing themselves of the charity, could only be surmised by the quality of the garments in which the children were dressed, the particulars of which were faithfully recorded ; the following being a sample, viz. :—

" 1741.—A male child, about two months old, with white dimity sleeves, lined with white, and tied with red ribbon."

" A female child, aged about six weeks, with a blue figured ribbon, and purple and white printed linen sleeves, turned up with red and white."

" A male child, about a fortnight old, very neatly dressed ; a fine holland cap, with a cambric border, white corded dimity sleeves, the shirt ruffled with cambric."

" A male child, a week old ; a holland cap, with a plain border, edged biggin and forehead-cloth, diaper bib, striped and flowered dimity mantle, and another holland one ; India dimity sleeves, turned up with stitched holland, damask waistcoat, holland ruffled shirt."

Sometimes the recording clerk was rather laconic and quaint in his descriptions : for instance, of one of the children he says, it had

"A paper on the breast—
Clout over the head."

Children received with Money.—After Parliament (frightened by the spirit of evil itself had raised) had deserted the Charity, the Governors were left to pursue, once more, their own course, and to adapt, if they thought fit, its administration to the more immediate objects of the Founder. This they were evidently desirous of doing, but the extravagancies caused by the "nationality" of their Institution for the period alluded to, had emptied the Exchequer of the Hospital, and the evils of the system had so offended the public, that much of the individual support which it previously received from charitable persons was withdrawn.

Their "poverty," perhaps not the "will" of the acting Governors, led them into an error of another kind, namely—a resolution to receive children with *money*, in addition to such other objects as the funds of the Hospital might enable them to maintain. It is a fact, much to be regretted, that for many years children were mysteriously received on payment of £100. without a knowledge of, or any clue being given to the parents from whom they sprung! The abuses which might, and no doubt did arise from this system, are so obvious as to need no comment.

It is due, however, to the Governors to say, that immediately after the funds of the charity had assumed a healthier state, they abolished altogether this more than questionable practice. At a Court of Governors, held on the 21st January, 1801, there being present several eminent lawyers, including Mr. (afterwards Baron) Garrow, and Sir Thomas Plumer (subsequently Master of the Rolls), it was resolved to rescind the obnoxious bye-law which originated so objectionable a system. The truth is, the matter was about to be brought to a legal issue, from the following circumstance : — The mother of a child which had been received under this rule, although a consenting party to the separation, afterwards repented, and, having discovered the residence of the nurse with whom it was placed in the country, practiced upon her an artifice by which she obtained possession of the child, and refused to relinquish her right. The Governors feeling themselves under an obligation to reclaim the child by exercising the powers which they conceived to be vested in them, took a high legal opinion, when they were advised, that owing to their departure in this respect from the spirit and letter of their charter, and the Act of Parliament confirming it, they had no chance of being protected in a court of law. *From this time, therefore, namely, January, 1801, no child has been received into the Hospital, either directly or indirectly, with any sum of money, large or small.*

The present practice.—The present mode of admitting children has prevailed for more than half a century, without those variations of principle and practice which characterized previous periods of the history of the Hospital. It cannot be better set forth than in the language of a report made to Parliament in 1836, by a commission appointed to enquire into the larger charities of London :—

" The present practice of the Governors is to decide each application for the admission of children on its own merits. There are, however, certain preliminary conditions required, the absence of any one of which is fatal to the petitioner's application, and subjects it to instant rejection, except in very peculiar cases. Thus it is required,

" 1. That the child shall be illegitimate, except the father be a soldier or sailor killed in the service of his country.*

" 2. That the child be born, and its age under twelve months.

" 3. That the petitioner shall not have made an application to any parish respecting its maintenance, or have been delivered in any parish workhouse.

" 4. That the petitioner shall have borne a good character previous to her misfortune or delivery.

" 5. That the father shall have deserted his offspring, and be not *forthcoming*, that is, not to be found, or compellable to maintain his child.

---

* No body of men could have been influenced by more noble and patriotic feelings on different occasions than the Governors of the Foundling Hospital. In 1761, during the war in Germany, also during the Continental war in 1794, and on the occasion of the battle of Waterloo, they freely opened their gates to the necessitous children of those who had fallen in the service of their country. Illegitimate children are now the sole objects of the Charity.

" Supposing, therefore, that it appears by the petition, and the petitioner's examination,* that the claim for admission is advanced in respect of an illegitimate child, of a hitherto respectable parent, not twelve months old, whose father has deserted it and is not forthcoming, and whose birth has not been taken cognizance of by any parish authorities, the petitioner is considered to have established a case for inquiry; and the " Enquirer " is directed to obtain information, both as to these and as to other circumstances in the case now to be stated, which differ from those above-mentioned in this respect, that none are absolutely required, and that they are all taken into consideration by the Governors, and influence their estimate of the merits of each application, according to the *degree* only in which they prevail in the individual one under consideration.

" Thus the petitioner's child acquires a stronger claim to admission, according to the degree in which it appears.

" 1. That the petitioner is poor, and has no relations able or willing to maintain her child.

" 2. That her delivery and shame are known to few persons, being either her relations or inmates of the house in which the circumstances occurred.

" 3. That in the event of the child being received, the petitioner has a prospect of preserving her station in society, and obtaining by her own exertions an honest livelihood.

---

* " No one can blame the total change of the plan, which for the last

" The most meritorious case, therefore, would be one in which a young woman, having no means of subsistence, except those derived from her own labour, and having no opulent relations, previously to committing the offence bore an irreproachable character, but yielded to artful and long-continued seduction, and an express promise of marriage ; whose delivery took place in secret, and whose shame was known to only one or two persons, as, for example, the medical attendant and a single relation ; and, lastly, whose employers or other persons were able and desirous to take her into their service, if enabled again to earn her livelihood by the reception of her child.

" This is considered the most eligible case, and others are deemed by the Governors as more or less so, in proportion as they approach nearer to or recede further from that above stated ; their great object being, as they allege, to fulfil to the utmost the benevolent views of the principal Founder of the Hospital, who, as appears by his petition for the charter, was chiefly solicitous that the mothers of illegitimate children should have other means within their reach of hiding their shame than the destruction of their miserable offspring, and thus they say they seek ' to hide the shame of the mother as well as to preserve the life of the child.' "

---

sixty years has been made, with whatever view, by adopting the rule to admit no child whose mother does not appear to be examined. "—*Lord Brougham's Letter to Sir Samuel Romilly on Charities.*

THE EXISTENCE OF THE CHARITY.

The first sympathies of the human heart are doubtless excited by the presence of misery, originating in what may be termed the *accidents* of life, unassisted either by the transgression or omission of the individual. Distress thus obtained, has at all times received, though not systematically, the compassionate alleviation which it requires. But there is misery of another class, which has its origin in the moral weaknesses of our nature : this, though more poignant than the former, inasmuch as it is followed by the bitterness of acknowledged transgression, did not in darker ages receive, because to human wisdom it did not seem to deserve, the commiseration of mankind. But the Christian religion, by its admirable precepts and influences, has imbued the social system of nations with a policy, which is founded on a compassionate estimate of the weaknesses of humanity, and a just measure of relief to voluntary repentance. This lesson of mercy was eminently taught by the Founder of Christianity himself, when he bade the Jew who was without sin cast the first stone at the repentant adultress, and then calmly dismissed her with the charge to *sin no more !* * It was not that her crime

---

* Moore's poetical paraphrase of this subject naturally recurs to the mind :—

E

was venial, but He who desired not the death of
a sinner, but rather that she should repent and
live, saw in this wretched criminal, sufficient of
remorse to be the object of a lesson to mankind,—
that the rigour of human law should not be exercised
without a humane regard to the circumstances under
which crime may have been committed, and to the
sincerity of the atonement which may have followed.

It may be asked, then, where is the man, imbued
with Christian charity, who is prepared to take up
the stone, and fling it at the poor victim of
unprincipled seduction and brutal desertion? Is he
ready to bear in like manner the consequences of
his own guilt, and to go down the stream of life
with her in her shattered bark? No: and yet
there are certain pseudo-moralists, afflicted with an
unfortunate obliquity of the mind's eye, who, rather
than succour the necessities of one whose misfortune
originated in evil, would hurl the offender headlong
into perdition. Alas! the descent from virtue to
vice is so easy, that but one step intervenes between

"Oh, woman! if by simple wile
   Thy soul has stray'd from honour's track.
'Tis mercy only can beguile,
   By gentle ways, the wand'rer back.

"The stain that on thy virtue lies,
   Wash'd by thy tears, may yet decay;
As clouds that sully morning skies,
   May all be wept in show'rs away.

"Go, go—be innocent, and live—
   The tongues of men may wound thee sore;
But heav'n in pity can forgive,
   And bids thee 'Go, and sin no more!'"

them: and often, when we think we are secure, our foot slips, and we are involved in all the misery and degredation of sin! This is the fate of us all: tis the fate of him who proudly glories in his own rectitude; for what is the moral history of a man's life? 'Tis but a succession from virtue to vice, from vice to repentance. Shall man, then, who is so weak as not to be able to sustain his own virtue, withhold from a wretched woman, who by wily arts has been deceived, that compassion for her error which he requires for himself? And yet, those who oppose an institution founded on such principles and practice as the Foundling Hospital is now conducted, answer by their conduct the very affirmative of this question. We ask in the language of an eminent writer,* " Have faults no extenuations? Is there no difference betwixt one propensely going out of the road, and continuing there through depravity of will,—and a hapless wanderer straying by delusion, and warily treading back her steps?" The latter are the peculiar objects of the Foundling Hospital; and what Christian—what man is there who will gainsay the humanity of such an institution?

But there are certain individuals who endeavour to smother their humanity under the plea, that the policy—*the good of society* as they term it—is against the existence of any institution which shall relieve distress arising out of an evil action.† Now it may

---

* Sterne, who preached a sermon for the charity, in the chapel of the Hospital, in 1761.

† If this doctrine were generally acted upon, what would become of the

be well to answer these rigid interpreters by enquiring, how far *the good of society* is injured by the institution of an asylum for the protection of infants, whose wretched parents, first straying by delusion, warily tread back their steps?

We know that *shame* is sometimes so powerful a monitor in the female breast, that it is impossible to resist its influence. Suppose then, the victim of seduction,—deceived, deserted, without even the shadow of hope in the distance to point to her relief:—suppose, we say, this wretched creature overtaken by despair, and, in a fit of madness, to become the murderess of her infant! we ask, how is the *good of society* answered by driving her to this desperate act? Would it not have been better secured by an opposite course? In the first place, by rescuing the infant from destruction, through the medium of some public asylum, it might be enabled hereafter to give its modicum of strength for the benefit of that public, through whose compassion it might have been saved. And secondly, by preserving the wretched parent from so desperate a crime, she might, by her penitence and future rectitude, have maintained the cause of virtue, and once more enjoyed the pleasure of reputation after having tasted the ill consequences of losing it.

But we will suppose that the delirium of her despair

---

numerous medical and surgical charities of the kingdom, which are half filled with cases originating in the weaknesses or vices of humanity. How many beds of such noble establishments as St. Bartholomew's, St. Thomas's, Guy's, &c., &c., would become vacant?

does not reach to so great a height : we will take it for granted, that nature asserts so powerfully her claims, that this victim of seduction is ready to brave all consequences for the preservation of her offspring. How can she do this ?—she dare not apply to her relations :—they would reject and despise her. Her seducer has placed himself out of the reach of the law, —she has no means within herself—no hope ! Being therefore unable to afford protection to her offspring in an *honest* way, she throws off for ever her remaining mantle of virtue and abandons herself to a prostituted life ? Is *the good of society* promoted by her swelling the awful lists of public prostitutes ? Is it promoted by her bringing up her child in the path of vice instead of virtue ? No. And yet we are told by these spurious moralists, that it is unwise to step in between a hapless female and the punishment of lasting infamy which they would allot to her offence.

> " Curse on the savage and unbending law
> Of stern society, that turns a speck
> In woman to an everlasting flaw !
> And far from whisp'ring us to save or check
> Her course in wantonness, bids us draw
> Round her, like wretches hov'ring round a wreck,
> All that the wave hath spar'd, to spoil and plunder,
> And sink the noble vessel farther under."

Many are the indirect testimonies given by men of talent in favour both of the policy and humanity towards which the objects of the Foundling Hospital are directed. Fielding, who had a profound knowledge of human nature and human action, puts into the mouth of Mr. Allworthy, in his inimitable novel of

"Tom Jones," the most benevolent and, at the same time, the most sensible reasons for sheltering and befriending the supposed mother of the little foundling; and in his parting admonition to her, makes the good man say, " I have talked thus to you child, not to insult you for what is past and irrecoverable, but to caution and strengthen you for the future. Nor should I have taken this trouble, but from some opinion of your good sense, notwithstanding the dreadful slip you have made, and from some hopes of your hearty repentance, which are founded on the openness and sincerity of your confession." And when her enemies would have sacrificed her to ruin and infamy, by a shameful correction in a bridewell, " so far " (says the author) " from complying with this their inclination,

---

The following verses from the pen of H. W. Freeland, Esq., may not unappropriately be here inserted.

O spurn her not ! a mother's care
  Her childhood never knew,
And she was once like angels fair,
  And innocent, and true.

O spurn her not ! for she had none
  A warning word to say ;
Of all the flock there was but one
  That e'er was known to stray.

When proud man errs, a world that's blind
  To justice and to truth,
Too quickly frames excuses kind
  For thoughtlessness and youth ;

When woman falls, her infamy
  A thousand lips proclaim,
And busy tongues seem pleas'd to be
  The heralds of her shame.

by which all hopes of reformation would have been abolished, and even the gate shut against her, if her own inclination should ever hereafter lead her to choose the road of virtue, Mr. Allworthy rather chose to encourage the girl to return thither by the only possible means ; *for* (he adds) *too true I am afraid it is, that many women have become abandoned, and have sunk to the last degree of vice, by being unable to retrieve the first slip.*"

In the same strain the celebrated Dr. Burn * laments the abandonment of erring females, by which (he says) " they become desperate and profligate, and are induced to make a trade of that vice, which at first was a pitiable weakness." Surely the testimony

---

Then pause, lest One that cannot err
　Should crush usurping pride,
And mercy, now withheld from her,
　Should be to you denied.

Goad not to acts of last despair,
　But kindly bid her live;
Most human 'tis to err—most fair
　And heavenly to forgive.

Pity her too confiding youth
　That early learn'd to stray,
And lead her back to holy truth
　And virtue's sacred way.

Though fall'n she looks from guilt and sin
　To mercy's throne above;
And lost on earth, is still within
　The pale of heavenly love.

* Author of " Burn's Justice."

of such men in favour of the preservation of God's creatures from destruction, is of infinitely greater value than all the theories of political economists !

The late Rev. Sydney Smith, who, from the office he held, as one of the preachers of the Chapel of the Hospital, was well acquainted with the "working" of it, thus writes :—

"A very unfounded idea exists in the minds of some men little acquainted with the principles on which we proceed, that the doors of this Hospital are flung open to the promiscuous reception of infants, and that every mother can here find an asylum for her offspring, whatever be her pretensions as a virtuous mother, an indigent mother, or a mother striving by every exertion of industry to give to her children creditable support. If this were so, this institution would aim directly, and in the most unqualified manner, at the destruction of two virtues on which the happiness of society principally depends—the affection of parents, and the virtue of women. We should be counteracting, under the name of charity, all those omnipotent principles of exertion founded on the love of offspring ; —we should be weakening that sacred resolution to watch, to toil, and to meet all dangers, to suffer all pains, rather than children should know the shadow of a grief, or endure but an instant of sorrow ;— we should be whispering into the ear of poverty the most pernicious of all precepts ;—we should be inviting them to relax from the noblest efforts, to blunt the finest feelings, and to disobey the highest commandments of Almighty God. My brethren, these things are not so : our zeal is combined with greater knowledge ; and experience has taught us, that the designs of the pious demand a circumspection not inferior to that with which the machinations of the wicked are pursued. No child drinks of our cup or eats of our bread whose reception, upon the whole, we are not certain to be more conducive than pernicious to the interests of religion and good morals. We hear no mother whom it would not be merciless and shocking to turn away ; we exercise the trust reposed in us with a trembling and sensitive conscience ; we do not think it enough to say, This woman is wretched, and betrayed, and forsaken ; but we calmly reflect if it be expedient that her tears should be dried up, her loneliness sheltered, and all her wants receive the ministration of charity. The object has uniformly been to distinguish between hardened guilt and the first taint of vice. By sheltering and protecting once, to reclaim for ever after, and not to doom to eternal infamy for one single stain of guilt.

" The fair and just way to estimate degrees of guilt is to oppose them to degrees of temptation ; and no one can know more perfectly than the conductors of this charity, the abominable artifices by which the poor women who come to them for relief have been ruined, and the cruelty with which they have been abandoned. My brethren, do not believe that these are the mere casualties of vice,

F

and the irregularities of passion, which, though
well governed in the main, degenerate into
occasional excess. The mothers whom we relieve
have been too often ruined by systematic profligacy
—by men, the only object and occupation of whose
life it is to discover innocence, and to betray it.
There are men in this great city who live only for
such a purpose, who are the greatest and most
dreadful curses that the earth carries upon its
surface. My dear brethren, if I were to show you
in this church the figure of a wretched woman,
a brutal, shameless creature, clothed in rags, and
mouldering with disease ;—if I were to tell you
she had once been good and happy, that she once
had that chance of salvation which we all have this
day ;—if I were to show you the man who had
doomed her to misery in this world, and to hell in
the world to come, what would your feelings be ?
If I were to bring you another as sick and as
wretched as her, and were to point out the same
man as the cause of her ruin, how would your
indignation rise ? But if I were to tell you that
the constant occupations of this man were to search
for innocence and to ruin it ; that he was a seducer
by profession ; that the only object for which he
existed was to gratify his infamous passions at
every expense of human happiness, would you not
say that his life was too bad for the mercy of
God ? If the earth were to yawn for him as it
yawned for Dathan and Abiram, is there one eye
would be lifted up to ask for mercy for his soul ?

It is from such wretches as these that we strive to rescue unhappy women, to bring them back to God, to secure them from the scorn of the world that would break their hearts, and drive them into the deepest gulf of sin. But this is not all : to the cruelty of seduction is generally added the baseness of abandoning its object,—of leaving to perish in rags and in hunger a miserable woman, bribed by promises and oaths of eternal protection and regard. Now, my brethren, let us be just even to sinners ; let us be merciful even to seducers in the midst of horror for their crimes ; let us fix before our eyes every circumstance that can extenuate them ; let us place by the side of the guilt the temptation, and judge them as we hope to be judged at a perilous season by the great Judge of us all. Let us call seduction the effect of youth and passion, still we have a right to expect all that compensation of good which youth and passion commonly afford, if we allow to them all the indulgence they usually require ; but what of youth or passion is there in forgetting the unprotected weakness of women—in starving a creature whom you have ruined—in flying from her for fear she should ask you for bread ? Does youth thus unite fervour with meanness ? Does it, without a single compensatory virtue, combine its own vices and the vices of every other period of life ? Is it violent and sordid, avaricious and impassioned, the slave of every other feeling, and the master of generous compassion alone ? This is not youth ;

this has nothing to do with the origin of life; it is cold and callous profligacy begun in brutal sensuality, fostered by irreligion, strengthened by association with bad men, and become so hardened, that it laughs at the very misery it creates. These are the feelings, and these the men, whose cruelty we are obliged to alleviate, and whose victims we are destined to save. Is there any friend to virtue, however rigid, who can say that such an application of charity, so scrupulous and so discriminating, is not a solid augmentation of human happiness? that it does not extend the dominion of the Gospel, and narrow the boundaries of sin? But let those who conceive that the claims even of such unhappy women should be rejected, consider what it is they do reject: they reject the weakness of sex; they are deaf to the voice of ruined innocence; they refuse assistance to youth, shuddering at the gulf of infamy; they would turn out an indigent mother to the merciless world, at a period when she demands all that charity can afford, or compassion feel! But whatever be the crimes of the parents, and whatever views different individuals may take of the relief extended to them, there is no man who thinks that the children should perish for their crimes, or that those shall be doomed to suffer any misery who can have committed no fault. Therefore this part of the institution is as free from the shadow of blame as every other part is free from the reality."

Sir Thomas Bernard, Baronet, who was for some

years Treasurer of the Hospital, writes as follows
in 1803*:—

"The preserving and educating so many children,
which without the Foundling Hospital would have
been lost to that society of which they are calculated
to become useful members, is certainly a great and
public benefit. The adoption of a helpless, unprotected
infant, the watching over its progress to maturity,
and fitting it to be useful to itself and others here,
and to attain eternal happiness hereafter, these are
no common or ordinary acts of beneficence; but their
value and their importance are lost, when compared
with the benefits which (without any prejudice to the
original objects of the Charity) the mothers derive
from this Institution, as it is at present conducted.
The preserving the mere vital functions of an infant
cannot be put in competition with saving from vice,
misery, and infamy, a young woman, in the bloom of
life, whose crime may have been a single and solitary
act of indiscretion. Many extraordinary cases of
repentance, followed by restoration to peace, comfort,
and reputation, have come within the knowledge of
the writer of this note. Some cases have occurred,
within his own observation, of wives happily placed,
the mothers of thriving families, who, but for the
saving aid of this Institution, might have become
the most noxious and abandoned prostitutes. Very
rare are the instances, none has come within
notice, of a woman relieved by the Foundling

---

* *Vide* Report of the Society for Bettering the Condition of the Poor.

Hospital, and not thereby preserved from a course of prostitution."

There are at present 460 children supported by the Hospital, from extreme infancy up to the age of fifteen. This is the maximum number for the maintenance of which the present funds can be made available. It is only therefore as vacancies occur by apprenticeship or death, reducing this number, that other children can be received. The average admissions per annum for the last five years was thirty-seven. The average number of applications for the admission of children was 206. Independently, therefore, of a principle of action which governs the Committee in the selection of cases, the limited means at their disposal, as compared with the claims upon them, furnishes of itself a safe-guard or guarantee against a too free administration of this, the most important branch of the establishment.

It has been said (and gravely, though ridiculously, charged against the Hospital) that the Governors are liable to be deceived, and that in some cases they have been imposed upon by designing persons. This may be so, it being the fate of all *human* institutions to be imperfect. Judges and juries are very often betrayed into error by false witnesses, but does any one pretend to assert that therefore, courts of justice are useless? If the duration of institutions, of whatever nature, was to depend upon the perfect integrity of their administration, it is to be feared that their existence would be short-lived indeed!

THE PRIVILEGES OF THE GOVERNORS.

There is a class of men with so little charity in their hearts, as to make it an incomprehensible matter to them how any individual can be found, in this mercenary world, to contribute either his time or money to benevolent purposes without some commensurate benefit to himself; but it is a fact, notwithstanding, that there is a large body of individuals (and miserable indeed would society be without such persons), who from the purest motives of Christian charity, are to be found dispensing the good with which God has blest them, for the benefit of their poorer sojourners in this world of sin and misery, divested entirely of self-interest. Of that number are the Governors of the Foundling Hospital! It is asserted without fear of contradiction, by one who has had for many years ample opportunity of ascertaining it, that there is not a charity in or out of the metropolis, more *disinterestedly* administered in the selection of its objects than this institution. It has become a *principle* (fully supported in *practice*), that no Governor shall interfere, either directly or indirectly, by recommendation or otherwise, in obtaining the admission of a child. No interest is exercised except what the abstract misery of the case on its presentation excites, and all extraneous support is set aside. The truth is, that the persons relieved are of that class who are unable to command patronage, or who dare not seek it lest their error and their misery should be betrayed!

This administration of an important branch of such an institution is thus asserted, because there is a "vulgar error" on the subject, namely—that the Governors have the privilege of *presenting* children, after the manner of other establishments; but a more unfounded statement never was erroneously conceived or ignorantly disseminated!

The pecuniary qualification of a Governor is a donation of fifty pounds. There are pews in the Chapel set apart for the accommodation of Governors and their families free of charge.

NAMING AND BAPTIZING OF THE CHILDREN.

It has been the practice of the Governors, from the earliest period of the Hospital to the present time, to name the children at their own will and pleasure, whether their parents should have been known or not.

At the baptism of the children first taken into the Hospital, which was on the 29th March, 1741, it is recorded, that "there was at the ceremony a fine appearance of persons of quality and distinction: his Grace the Duke of Bedford, our President, their Graces the Duke and Duchess of Richmond, the Countess of Pembroke, and several others, honouring the children with their names, and being their sponsors."

Thus the register of this period presents the courtly names of Abercorn, Bedford, Bentinck, Montague, Marlborough, Newcastle, Norfolk, Pomfret, Pembroke, Richmond, Vernon, &c., &c., as well as those of numerous other living individuals, great and small, who at that time took an interest in the establishment. When these names were exhausted, the authorities stole those of eminent deceased personages, their first attack being upon the church. Hence we have a Wickliffe, Huss, Ridley, Latimer, Laud, Sancroft, Tillotson, Tennison, Sherlock, &c., &c. Then come the mighty dead of the poetical race, viz.—Geoffrey Chaucer, William Shakspeare, John Milton, &c. Of the philosophers, Francis Bacon stands pre-eminently conspicuous. As they proceeded, the Governors were more warlike in their notions, and brought from their graves Philip Sidney, Francis Drake, Oliver Cromwell, John Hampden, Admiral Benbow, and Cloudesley Shovel. A more peaceful list followed this, viz.—Peter Paul Rubens, Anthony Vandyke, Michael Angelo, and Godfrey Kneller ; William Hogarth, and Jane, his wife, of course not being forgotten. Another class of names was borrowed from popular novels of the day, which accounts for Charles Allworthy, Tom Jones, Sophia Western, and Clarissa Harlowe. The gentle Isaac Walton stands alone. The last child received under the parliamentary system alluded to at page 14 was named *Kitty Finis.*

So long as the admission of children was confined within reasonable bounds, it was an easy matter to find names for them ; but during the " parliamentary era" of the Hospital, when its gates were thrown open to all comers, and each day brought its regiment of *infantry* to the establishment, the Governors were sometimes in difficulties; and when this was the case, they took a zoological view of the subject, and named them after the creeping things and beasts of the earth, or created a nomenclature from various handicrafts or trades.

In 1801, the hero of the Nile and some of his friends honoured the establishment with a visit, and stood sponsors to several of the children. The names given on this occasion were Baltic Nelson, William and Emma Hamilton, Hyde Parker, &c.

Up to a very late period the Governors were sometimes in the habit of naming the children after themselves or their friends; but it was found to be an inconvenient and objectionable course, inasmuch as when they grew to man or woman-hood, they were apt to lay claim to some affinity of blood with their nomenclators. The present practice therefore is, for the Treasurer to prepare a list of ordinary names, by which the children are baptized.

THE NURSING OF THE CHILDREN.

There can be no doubt that as the object of an institution of this nature is to save life, its managers should take all reasonable means for effecting such a desideratum. It is with this intention that the present Governors invariably obtain for the infants falling under their charitable care, *wet nurses*, unless it happens (which is rarely the case) that the age of a child renders such assistance unnecessary. The result, therefore, of this course is much more favourable than that adopted at the outset of the establishment.

In considering the question of mortality, the children of the Hospital should be classed under two heads, namely :—1st, those under the age of three years in the *country*, and 2ndly, those from three to fifteen in *London*.

With respect to the former, the chances against rearing many of them are very great, and for these reasons. The mothers of the infants (who for the most part are very young) being desirous of " hiding their shame " from their relatives, or those with whom they may happen to be placed, manage by contrivances and artifices to prevent a knowledge of their imprudence until it can no longer be concealed. The writer has known many instances where girls (for their youth justifies the designation) have been living with their mothers, with whom they have been in constant intercourse, and even sleeping in the same bed, and yet have contrived to hide from their parents the fact of their unfortunate condition till the moment of confinement. In the same manner servants manage to undergo the labours of their office, and contrive to elude the observation of their mistresses, till the instant of giving birth to a child. The unnatural distortions of body by which their

secret is preserved, are accompanied by anxieties of
mind which does not arise only from the dread of
discovery. The prospect before her is dreary enough,
but the retrospect is perhaps worse. " She finds
herself " (says the late Rev. John Hewlett), " the
victim of treachery and voluptuousness, where she
fondly hoped to be the object of pure and individual
love, and at a time when the languor of the body
and the growing anxiety of the mind powerfully
claim, and in general receive, additional tenderness,
she is obliged to endure the severest affliction that
fear could imagine, or unkindness produce." Can it
be wondered at therefore, that an infant born under
such circumstances should be deficient in those
physical developments which otherwise it might have
possessed ? But this is not all. The same powerful
motive which prompted her first desire to conceal her
disgrace, leads her to seek the only other opportunity
she has of ensuring such concealment, namely—by
putting her infant away from her, as soon after
its birth as possible, to some nurse, who under a
promise of payment, which the mother is unable to
fulfil, engages to take upon herself the duties of
the parent, duties which in nine cases out of ten
she neglects to perform in a satisfactory manner.
Beginning life with such opposing contingencies,
and thus neglected, the infant is admitted into the
Foundling Hospital. " At least one-fifth of those
admitted during the last nine years " (says the
examining medical officer) " have been in such a
miserable state of emaciation, as to make it doubtful

if they could be reared at all, and of those presented in tolerable health, many receive a serious check from the change of nurse, condition, and other circumstances attending their admission. These infants are presented at all ages, from one to twelve months, and have been mostly exposed to all the injurious consequences arising from insufficient nursing and improper diet ; the greater number have not had the breast at all, and I have generally found on enquiry, that those who have had the advantage of a wet nurse, have been fed at the same time with spoon food."

The general health of the children within the walls of the Hospital is remarkably good; and with the exception of occasional epidemic visitations, they have been singularly free from the acute forms of disease to which children in general are so liable.

Perhaps the healthiness of the locality could not be better exemplified than by this fact—that several adult foundlings, who, from some organic defect, have from time to time become chargeable to the Hospital for life, and have scarcely ever quitted the walls of the building, have lived to a very advanced period—some dying between the ages of seventy and eighty years, and others between eighty and ninety.*

---

* "Now that there seems to be so great a desire to move to the west-end of the metropolis, either to Belgravia or Tyburnia, it may be advisable to inform Her Majesty's subjects, that there is no healthier part of this great town than the space contained within the following boundaries, viz. :— Holborn and New Oxford Street, on the south ; the New Road, on the north ; Grays Inn, on the east ; and Tottenham Court Road, on the west ;

THE DISPOSAL OF THE CHILDREN.

The children are generally disposed of by *apprenticeship :* the girls at the age of fifteen to domestic service, for a term of five years, and the boys at the age of fourteen as mechanics, for a term of seven years—some of the boys, however, having a knowledge of music, volunteer into the bands of the army or navy ; many of them were in the Crimea during the Russian War.

THE REVENUE OF THE HOSPITAL.

There is much misconception and misunderstanding on the part of the public on this head.

In the memoir of Captain Coram, it is clearly shewn that what property he had acquired, was consumed in the pursuit of his philanthropic projects, and that he had no wealth by which to endow, even in a limited degree, an institution of this nature,

----

—which space contains within it the twenty-two squares or open spaces, following :—

" 1. Gray's Inn, 2. its Squares, 3. its Gardens ; 4. Foundling Hospital, 5. its Gardens ; 6. Burial Ground ; 7. Mecklenburgh Square ; 8. Regent Square ; 9. Argyle Square ; 10. Red Lion Square ; 11. Queen Square ; 12. Bloomsbury Square ; 13. Bedford Square ; 14. Russell Square ; 15. Torrington Square ; 16. Woburn Square ; 17. Gordon Square ; 18. Tavistock Square ; 19. Euston Square ; 20. Burton Crescent ; 21. University College Grounds ; 22. Brunswick Square.

" If this were in Paris, it would be called " *Le Quartier des Carré's.*" The streets generally run at right angles to each other. It is a gravelly soil, and the spring water excellent."—*The Builder.*

being himself a recipient of charity for the last two
years of his life. The Hospital had nothing,
therefore, to depend upon at its commencement, but
the eleemosynary aid of the public, either in the
form of donations or legacies ; and what permanent
revenue it now has, may be ascribed to the fortuitous
policy of the early Governors and the provident care
of their successors. Thus the Governors in 1741,
being in pursuit of a salubrious site for erecting an
Hospital, fixed upon certain fields in the neighbourhood
of London, deriving their name from " Lamb's
Conduit "* (in extent fifty-six acres), belonging to the
Earl of Salisbury, who agreed to sell them to the
charity for £5,500. The whole tract of land was
purchased out of casual benefactions and legacies,
not because the charity required it for its then
purposes, but because the Earl would not sell any
fractional part of it. As London increased, it
approached this property, and the Governors were
induced fifty-five years after to turn that to the
pecuniary advantage of the charity, which its early
managers had not the remotest idea would have ever
become otherwise beneficial than as guaranteeing the
healthy condition of the children. From this
accidental circumstance, the Governors derive, from
ground rents alone, an annual income equal to the
purchase-money! This income is secured by leases

---

* The lands of the Hospital in the parish of St. Pancras belonged to the
Prior of the House of The Salvation of the Mother of God, of the order of
the Carthusians :—the same was granted by Queen Elizabeth, in 1532,
to Vaughan and Ellis.

of ninety-nine years duration, of which there is an average unexpired term of thirty-five years, so that until that period, the income from this source must remain the same.

Some imaginative persons have invested the Hospital already with the property in which it has only a remote reversionary interest, and they unwisely withhold their charitable hands, not because they disapprove of the institution, but because it is already so rich ! No charity can be rich unless it has a surplus revenue after every reasonable opportunity has offered for disposing of it upon the objects for whose benefit it was created. This is not the case with the Foundling Hospital. " It confines itself " (says Bishop Thirlwall) " to a particular class of cases—one, however, which is unhappily so large, that it constantly overgrows the means of relief." It should be understood therefore, that to these ground-rents, and the interest of certain stock, which has been nursed by the great care of the Guardians of the charity, to the Pew Rents and contributions at the chapel doors and other such casualties, the Hospital is wholly dependent for support, and will be so for nearly forty years to come.

The walls of the building present, it is true, a goodly array of tablets, noting considerable bene-factions and legacies, but it should be recollected that the greater part of this money was swallowed up in the vortex caused by Parliamentary interference, and that only during the last sixty years have the

Governors been able to lay up for the Hospital a pecuniary foundation.

Of those who were early benefactors, the name of Omychund, a black merchant of Calcutta, should be specially mentioned. He bequeathed to the Foundling and Magdalen Hospitals, 37,500 current rupees, to be equally divided; but unfortunately a portion only of this munificent legacy could be extracted from the grasp of Huzzorimal, his executor, notwithstanding the zealous interference of Warren Hastings., Esq., the Governor-General, and other eminent functionaries.

The following is a legacy of another kind. The testator was one Shirley, of Stratford, in Essex.

"The whole of my Dramatic Works, consisting of nine Tragedies, one Comedy, and five smaller productions, I bequeath to the Governors of the Foundling Hospital, in trust for that greatly useful Institution, hoping their being enabled to get them performed, unaltered or mutilated, in one of the London Theatres, they being certainly not inferior to any set of such performances produced at the present age ; and should they be acted, I request the repayment out of the profits to all subscribers to me, which can amount to but a small sum of money."

In 1759, William Williams, Esq., who possessed property in Jamaica, bequeathed the same to certain persons " *in trust to sell the same, together with all and every the Negro, Mulatto, and other slaves whatsoever to me belonging, with their future offspring, issue, or increase, and to pay the net proceeds to the Treasurer of the Foundling Hospital.*" His next bequest is as follows :—"*Item, I give and bequeath to that most abandonedly wicked, vile, detestable rogue and impostor, who hath assumed, and now does, or lately did go by the name of Gersham Williams, pretending to be a son of mine, one shilling only, to buy him an halter, wherewith to hang himself, being what he hath for a long, long, very long while past meritted and deserved from the law of the hands of the hangman, for his great and manifold villanies.*"

At the demise of his reputed father, this " Gersham Williams," made many attempts to compromise matters with the Governors of the Hospital regarding the legacy, but he proved a slippery character, and failed in his object. The legacy yielded to the charity £5563.

THE BENEVOLENT FUND.

This Fund was set on foot in the year 1845, on this humane principle, viz. :—That the helplessness of old age, especially when accompanied by an irreproachable life, was as worthy an object of compassion and amelioration as the helplessness of infancy, and that sickness, unprovoked by intemperance or other misconduct, deserved in the after life of the objects of the charity, as much alleviation as it received in the days of their youth. In fact, that as the Institution rescued them in childhood from want, or from the cold and compulsory charity of a parish workhouse, so in old age or sickness should it extend its merciful hand for the same object.

The Fund is dispensed by granting weekly allowances to the aged and infirm, and by affording temporary relief to the distressed.

It is wholly supported by subscription, the revenues of the Hospital not being applicable for the purpose.

THE HOSPITAL BECOMES ASSOCIATED WITH THE ARTS.

Sir Robert Strange, in his " Enquiry into the Rise and Establishment of the Royal Academy of Arts," makes the following remark :—

" The donations in painting, which several artists presented to the *Foundling Hospital*, were among the first objects of this nature which had engaged the attention of the public. The artists observing the effect that these paintings produced, came, in the year 1760, to a resolution to try the fate of an Exhibition of their works. This effort had its desired effect : the public were entertained, and the artists were excited to emulation."

And, again, in his " Conduct of the Royal Academicians," he says—

"Accident has often been observed to produce what the utmost efforts of industry have failed to accomplish ; and something of this kind seems to have happened here. As liberty has ever been considered the friend and parent of the Fine Arts, it is natural for their professors to revere the memory of all those who were the champions and assertors of that invaluable blessing, particularly those of our own country : on this principle it was, that the artists we are now speaking of, had an Annual Meeting at the *Foundling Hospital*, to commemorate the landing of King William. To this charity, several of their body had made donations in Painting, Sculpture, &c., which, being accessible to the public, made those artists more generally known than others, and this circumstance it was, that first suggested an Exhibition—which was no sooner proposed than approved. The committee, consequently, who were the proposers, received directions to issue proper notices of the intention. The performances of many ingenious men, hitherto unknown, were received, and on the 21st day of April, 1760, an Exhibition was opened in the great room belonging to the Society of Arts, Manufactures, and Commerce, in the Strand ; on which it will be sufficient to observe, that the success was equal to the most sanguine expectations ; the public were pleased and the artists applauded ; those already known received additional reputation, and such as were not, became the immediate acquaintance of the public."

Edwards, also, in his " Anecdotes of Painters," speaking of the unsuccessful attempts made to form an Academy, says—

" Although these endeavours of the artists had not succeded, they were far from being so discouraged as not to continue their meetings, as well as their studies ; and the next effort they made towards acquiring the attention of the public, was connected with the *Foundling Hospital.*

" This institution, so humane in its primitive intention, whatever may be thought of its effects, was incorporated by charter, dated 1739. A few years after that period, the present building was erected ; but as the income of the charity could with no propriety be expended on decorations, many of the principal artists of that day voluntarily exerted their talents for the purpose of ornamenting several of the apartments of the Hospital, which otherwise must have remained without decoration. The pictures thus produced, and generously given, were permitted to be seen by any visitor, upon proper application. The spectacle was so new that it made a considerable impression on the public, and the favorable reception these works experienced, impressed the artists with an idea of forming a public exhibition."

A more recent writer has said, " that it is within the walls of the *Foundling* the curious may contemplate the state of British Art, previously to the epoch when George the Third, first countenanced the historical talent of West."

William Hogarth, the celebrated painter, was

foremost amongst those who first cordially co-operated in forwarding the views of the Founder of the Hospital. In the charter for its in-corporation, he appears as one of its constituent members, under the denomination of " a Governor and Guardian," along with a host of other " trusty and well-beloved subjects" of his Majesty George the Second.

Nor did Hogarth hold this appointment to be merely nominal, for we find him subscribing his money, and attending the courts or general meetings at the Hospital, as one of its active members, and joining heartily in carrying out the designs of his friend, the venerable Founder.

The charter of the Hospital authorized the Governors to appoint persons to ask alms on behalf of the charity and to receive subscriptions; and the first artistical work of Hogarth in aid of this object, was to prepare a " head piece" to a power of attorney drawn up for the purpose: a copy of which head piece is annexed, taken from the original plate in the possession of the Hospital.

The principal figure is that of Captain Coram himself, with the Charter under his arm. Before him the beadle carries an infant, whose mother having dropped a dagger with which she might have been momentarily tempted to destroy her child, kneels at his feet, while he, with that benevolence with which his countenance is so eminently marked, bids her be comforted, for her babe will be nursed and protected. On the dexter side of the print, is a new born infant

left close to a stream of water which runs under the arch of a bridge. Near a gate on a little eminence in the pathway above, a woman leaves another child to the casual care of the next person who passes by. In the distance is a village with a church. In the other corner are three boys coming out of a door, with the king's arms over it, with emblems of their future employment; one of them poises a plummet, a second holds a trowel, and a third, whose mother is fondly pressing him to her bosom, has in his hand a card for combing wool. The next group, headed by a lad elevating a mathematical instrument, are in sailors' jackets and trousers. Those on their right hand, one of whom has a rake, are in the uniform of the school. The attributes of the three little girls in the foreground—a spinning wheel, a sampler and broom—indicate female industry and ingenuity.

It should be remarked that the designs of the Hospital, foreshadowed by this interesting engraving, did not come into actual operation till two years afterwards.

In May, 1740, that is, seven months after the granting of the Charter, at the Annual Court, "Mr. Folkes acquainted the Governors, that Mr. Hogarth had presented a whole length picture of Mr. Coram, for this Corporation to keep in memory of the said Mr. Coram's having solicited, and obtained His Majesty's Royal Charter for this Charity." Writing of himself some years afterwards, Hogarth says:—

"The portrait which I painted with most pleasure, and in which I particularly wished to excel. was that of Captain Coram for the *Foundling Hospital;* and " (he adds in allusion to his detractors as a portrait painter) "if I am so wretched an artist as my enemies assert, it is somewhat strange that this, which was one of the first I painted the size of life, should stand the test of twenty years' competition, and be generally thought the best portrait in the place, notwithstanding the first painters in the kingdom exerted all their talents to vie with it.*

Hogarth is said to have displayed no little vanity regarding his pretensions as a portrait painter. In proof of this, it is related of him, that being at dinner with Dr. Cheselden, and some other company, he was informed that John Freke, Surgeon of St. Bartholomew's Hospital, had asserted in Dick's Coffee House, that Greene was as eminent in composition as Handel. " That fellow, Freke," cried Hogarth, " is always shooting his bolt absurdly one way or another. Handel is a giant in music, Greene only a light Florimel kind of composer." " Aye, but " said the other, " Freke declared you were as good a portrait painter as Vandyck." " There he was in the right," quoth Hogarth, " and so I m,a give me but my time and let me choose my subject."

In March, 1741, the Governors resolved to commence upon the good purposes of their Charter,

---

* The rival portraits here alluded to are, George the Second, Patron of the Foundation, by Shackleton; Lord Dartmouth, one of the Vice-Presidents, by Mr. Reynolds (afterwards Sir Joshua); Taylor White, Treasurer of the Hospital, in crayons, by Cotes; Mr. Milner and Mr. Jacobson, by Hudson ; Dr. Mead by Ramsay ; Mr. Emmerson, by Highmore; and Francis Fauquier, Esq., by Wilson.

but not being able to obtain a suitable building, they took houses in Hatton Garden, near the Charity School, and opened them as receptacles and nurseries for Infants. In the minutes of that month is the following entry :—

" Mr. Taylor White acquainted the Committee that Mr. Hogarth had painted a Shield, which was put up over the door of this Hospital, and presented the same to this Hospital."

This shield, or sign, has not been preserved, nor is there any record of its design, but it is not improbable that it was an emblematical sketch similar in character, if not actually the same, as the Arms of the Hospital presented to the Court of Governors, by the Authorities of the Heralds' College, in 1747, and which is said by Nichols, in his Biographical Anecdotes, to have been designed by Hogarth. The technical description of these Arms is as follows, viz. :

" Party per fesse, Azure & Vert, a young child lying naked and exposed, extending its right hand proper. In chief a Crescent Argent between two Mullets of six points Or ; and for a Crest on a Wreath of the Colours, a Lamb Argent, holding in its mouth a Sprig of Thyme proper, supported on the dexter side by a terminal figure of a Woman full of Nipples proper, with a Mantle Vert, the term Argent being the emblem of Liberty, represented by Britannia holding in her right hand upon a staff proper, a Cap Argent, and habited in a Vest Azure, girt with belt Or, the under garment Gules." Motto " Help."

In 1740, the Governors of the Charity commenced

I

erecting on the land they had purchased the present
Building, the western wing of which was finished and
inhabited in 1745. It was at this period that Hogarth
contemplated the adornment of its walls with works
of Art, with which view he solicited and obtained the
co-operation of some of his professional brethren.
At a Court of Governors, held on the 31st December,
1746, Hogarth and Rysbrach, the sculptor, being present
as Governors of the Hospital, — "The Treasurer
acquainted this General Meeting that the following
Gentlemen, Artists, had severally presented, and
agreed to present, performances in their different
professions, for ornamenting this Hospital, viz.: Mr.
Francis Hayman, Mr. James Wills, Mr. Joseph
Highmore, Mr. Thomas Hudson, Mr. Allan Ramsay,
Mr. George Lambert, Mr. Samuel Scott, Mr. Peter
Monamy, Mr. Richard Wilson, Mr. Samuel Whale,
Mr. Edward Hately, Mr. Thomas Carter, Mr. George
Moser, Mr. Robert Taylor, and Mr. George Pyne.
Whereupon this General Meeting elected, by ballot,
the said Mr. Francis Hayman, Mr. James Wills,
Mr. Joseph Highmore, Mr. Thomas Hudson, Mr.
Allan Ramsay, Mr. George Lambert, Mr. Samuel
Scott, Mr. Peter Monamy, Mr. Richard Wilson, Mr.
Samuel Whale, Mr. Edward Hately, Mr. Thomas
Carter, Mr. George Moser, Mr. Robert Taylor, and
Mr. John Pyne, Governors and Guardians of this
Hospital.

" *Resolved*,—

"That the said Artists, and Mr. Hogarth, Mr.
Zinke, Mr. Rysbrach, and Mr. Jacobson, or any

three or more of them, be a Committee to meet annually on the 5th of November, to consider of what further ornaments may be added to this Hospital, without any expense to the charity."

Whether these artists were previously associated as a Society elsewhere for the promotion of the Arts, or for conviviality, does not appear, or whether they began to form themselves from this time and out of this occasion, cannot be determined, but it seems probable that they were part of a Society alluded to by Edwards, who says " of the Dilettante Society, the author is not sufficiently informed to give a perfect account, and therefore can only relate the following circumstances. Its original institution was prior to either of those already mentioned. It commenced upon political principles, and, as far as it was then known to the public, was not approved, being considered as rather a disaffected assembly. But they soon changed the object of their meetings and turned their attention to the encouragement of the Arts, and made some attempts to assist in the establishment of a public Academy."

Assuming that the artists who thus proposed to hold an annual meeting at the Hospital, belonged to the Dilettante Society, it may be said that whatevever their previous objects or bias might have been, their present purpose, notwithstanding the ominousness of the day fixed on for their meetings (viz.: the 5th of November), originated in as harmless a conspiracy as could be devised, that of plotting for the advancement of the Arts, and of a public charity.

It seems that these meetings, which commenced with the modest suggestion " that any three or more of them be a Committee," grew so mightily, that that which was intended to be a mere matter of business, ended (as most associations of Englishmen do) in an occasion of conviviality, and that on the 5th of November of each succeeding year, and for many years, the artists of the day, and the patronizers of the Arts, dined at the Hospital.*

In the meantime, the donations in Painting, &c., the result of these meetings, increased, and " being exhibited to the public, drew a daily crowd of spectators in their splendid equipages ; and a visit to the Foundling became the most fashionable morning lounge in the Reign of George II. The *eclat* thus excited in favor of the Arts, suggested the annual exhibition of the united artists, which institution was the precursor of the Royal Academy."†

Hogarth was not only the principal contributor, but the leader of his brethren in all that related to ornamenting the Hospital, and therefore, it is as much due to his benevolence and generosity, as to his distinguished talents, that his further connexion with the institution should receive special notice in this compilation.

At a Court of Governors on the 9th of May, 1750 (Hogarth being present),

---

* It appears by a document headed " *Delettante, Virtuosi, Feast*," that no less than 154 persons, more or less distinguished, dined at the Hospital on the 5th November, 1757.

† Vide *Catalogue Raisonnee* of West's pictures.

"The Treasurer acquainted the General Court, that Mr. Hogarth had presented the Hospital with the remainder of the tickets Mr. Hogarth had left, for the chance of the picture he had painted, of *The March to Finchley*, in the time of the late Rebellion; and that the fortunate number for the said picture being among those tickets, the Hospital had received the said picture.

" *Resolved*,—

"That the thanks of this General Court be given to Mr. Hogarth, for the said benefaction; which the Vice-President accordingly did."

In the "General Advertiser" of the 1st of May, 1750, the same circumstance is thus related:—

"Yesterday Mr. Hogarth's subscription was closed, 1843 chances being subscribed for, Mr. Hogarth gave the remaining 167 chances to the Foundling Hospital, and the same night delivered the picture to the Governors."

Ireland, in his Illustrations of Hogarth, remarks as follows on this subject.—

"By the fortunate number being among those presented to a charity, which he so much wished to serve, the artist was highly gratified. In a private house, it would have been in a degree secluded from the public, and by the lapse of time, have been transferred to those who could not appreciate its merit, and from either negligence or ignorance, might have been destroyed by damp walls, or effaced from the canvass by picture cleaners. Here, it was likely. to remain a permanent and honourable

testimony of his talents and liberality. Notwithstanding all this, Hogarth soon after waited upon
the Treasurer of the Hospital, and acquainted him
that if the Trustees thought proper, they were at
liberty to dispose of the picture by auction. His
motive for giving this permission it is not easy to
assign, it might have originated in a desire to
enrich a foundation, which had his warmest wishes,
or a natural, though ill-judged ambition to have
his greatest work in the possession of some who
had a collection of the old masters, with whom
he in no degree dreaded a competition. Whether
his mind was actuated by these, or other causes,
it is not important; certain it is, that his opinion
changed, he requested the trustees would not
dispose of it, and never afterwards consented to
the measure he himself had originally proposed.
The late Duke of Ancaster's father wished to
become a purchaser, and once offered the trustees
three hundred pounds for it. I have been told,
that a much larger sum was since proffered by
another gentleman."

It is related in the Gentleman's Magazine, on
the authority of an anonymous writer, " that a *Lady*
was the possessor of the fortunate number, and
intended to present it to the Foundling Hospital.
But that some person having suggested what a
door would be open to scandal, were any of her
sex to make such a present, it was given to
Hogarth, on the express condition that it should
be presented in his own name."

The next work which Hogarth presented, was "Moses before Pharaoh's Daughter." This was painted expressly for the Hospital, and appears to have originated in a conjoint agreement, between Hayman, Highmore, Wills, and himself, that they should each fill up one of the compartments of the Court Room with pictures, uniform in size, and of suitable subjects taken from Scripture.

The Hospital had thus obtained from Hogarth, a picture in each of the styles of painting which he had attempted, and it may be said, without fear of contradiction, that the best specimens of those styles are within its walls.

It is a somewhat singular circumstance, that as Hogarth throughout his life had uniformly opposed the establishment of a Public Academy of Arts, he should, by the very course he pursued in encouraging and concentrating at the Foundling Hospital an exhibition of the talents of British artists, have himself promoted a consummation of the object which he had all along deprecated. "In consequence," says Nichols, "of the public attention bestowed upon the paintings presented to the Foundling Hospital by Hogarth, the academy in St. Martin's Lane, began to form themselves into a more important body, and to teach the arts under regular professors. But, extraordinary as it may appear, this scheme was so far from being welcomed by Hogarth, as indicative of a brighter era in the Fine Arts, that he absolutely discouraged it, as tending to allure many young men into a profession in which they would not be able to support themselves, and at the same time to degrade what ought to be a liberal profession, into a merely mechanical one."

In the year 1760 the Hospital had grown to such an extent as to embrace within its arms several thousands of Children, so that the Governors were obliged to open Branch Establishments in the Country to receive them. One of these establishments was at Ackworth, in Yorkshire. At this place the children were usefully employed in the manufacture of cloth.* This led some of the artists to the benevolent and enthusiastic idea of promoting the good of the charity by appearing at their Festival in 1761, in clothing made by these children.

---

* One of the schemes for employing the children was the erection of a cotton machine invented by *Lewis Paul*, for whom Dr. Johnson framed a letter to the Duke of Bedford, President of the Hospital, on the subject,—of which the following is a copy :—

" My Lord,

"As beneficence is never exercised but at some expense of ease and leisure, your Grace will not be surprised that you are subjected, as the general Guardian of deserted infants, and protector of their Hospital, to intrusion and importunity, and you will pardon those who intend, though perhaps unskilfully, the promotion of the charity, the impropriety of their address for the goodness of their intention. I therefore take the liberty of proposing to your Grace's notice a machine for spinning cotton, of which I am the inventor and proprietor, as proper to be erected in the Foundling Hospital, its structure and operation being such that a mixed number of the children, from five to fourteen years, may be enabled by it to earn their food and clothing. In this machine, thus useful, and thus appropriated to the public, I hope to obtain from Parliament, by your Grace's recommendation, such a right as shall be thought due to the inventor.

"I know, my Lord, that every project must encounter opposition, and I would not encounter it, but that I think myself able to surmount it.

The following document is confirmatory of this interesting circumstance, and as evidence of the earnestness of the artists in this step, there is extant a letter dated 15th December, 1760, from the Rev. Dr. Lee, the indefatigable Governor of the Hospital at Ackworth, in which he says to the Treasurer in London, " Mr. Paine has wrote about clothing for the artists of the Turk's Head Club, and I should be glad to know if the twenty you speak of are not the same he writes about, and says will be in number sixty in a little time. He writes in the name of those gentlemen who will honour us with an uniform against their next Annual Meeting. I am to send him patterns of colours, but hope he'll choose that of your coat or something

---

Mankind has prejudices against every new undertaking which are no always prejudices of ignorance. He that only doubts what he does not know, may be satisfied by testimony, at least, by that of his own eyes ; but a projector, my Lord, has more dangerous enemies—the envious and the interested, who will neither hear reasons nor see facts, and whose animosity is more vehement as their conviction is more strong.

" I do not implore your Grace's patronage for a work existing only in possibility ; I have a machine erected, which I am ready to exhibit to the view of your Grace, or of any proper judge of mechanical performances whenever you shall be pleased to nominate. I shall decline no trial ; I shall seek no subterfuge ; but shall shew, not by argument, but practical experience, that what I have here promised will be easily performed.

" I am an old man, oppressed with many infirmities, and therefore cannot pay that attendance which your Grace's high quality demands, and my respect would dictate ; but whenever you shall be pleased to assign me an audience, I shall explain my design with the openness of a man who desires to hide nothing, and receive your Grace's commands with the submission which becomes,

My Lord,
Your Grace's most obedient
and most humble servant.

K

near it, because the deep coppers, from the nature
of the dye, render the wool too tender for the
spinning of our young artists to make any moderate
profit.   Of this you'll please to give a hint, as it
may not be so proper to insert it in my letter to him,
which probably he will show to his brethren."

"Turk's Head Tavern, December 7, 1760.
"We whose names are hereunto subscribed, do agree
to appear next 5th November, at the Artists' Feast,
at the Foundling Hospital, in Lamb's Conduit Fields,
in a suit of clothes manufactured by the children of
the Hospital, at Ackworth, in Yorkshire, to be all of
one colour and that they be made in Yorkshire.

Chrisr. Seaton, John Seaton, Jerh. Meyer, John
Gwynn, Wm. Chambery, Edwd. Rooker, Richd. Dalton,
W. Tyler, Jas. Paine, Js. McArdell, K. Coase, W. H.
Spang, Saml. Wale, Fra. Milner Newton, Nath. Honey,
G. M. Moser, J. Reynolds, T. Hayman, T. White, G.
Whatley, P. Sandby, T. Major, Thos. Brand, C. Hollis,
R. Hayward, Josh. Wilton, John Lockman, Richd. Yeo,
R. Wilson, Thos. Chambers, Wm. Ryland, Henry
Morland, Richd. Francklin, George Evans, L. D.
Roubiliac, John Lockman (for Mr. William Deard, at
his request), Mr. Dubiggan, Wm. Fletcher, S. Ravenet,
Frs. Reibenstein, W. Thomson."

At what precise period these meetings of the artists
at the Hospital ceased is not known, but there is no
doubt that as the Royal Academy, which was founded
in 1768, became established and consolidated the

convivial presence of its members was transferred to a more appropriate arena. The " Gentleman's Magazine," of the 5th November, 1763, thus testifies that up to that period the meetings were still continued.

"The Artists of London and Westminster held their Anniversary at the Foundling Hospital in commemoration of the day, and were entertained by the children with an anthem. A blind boy performed on the organ, and a little girl of five years of age the solo part of the vocal music."

Charles Lamb, in one of his critical essays, remarks that Hogarth seemed to take particular delight in introducing *Children* into his works.

As evidence that this characteristic was not the mere ideality of a painter, but emanated from that generous heart which guided his actions, the following anecdote of this extraordinary man is recorded.

It was the practice at this period, of the Hospital (as indeed it is at the present time) to nurse the Children of the establishment in the country till about three years of age, by distributing them amongst cottagers in certain districts, superintended by competent authorities in the neighbourhood.

These authorities formerly performed their interesting office *gratuitously*, and they consisted of resident gentry or ladies. In or about the year 1760, the Governors at the request of Hogarth, sent several of these infants to Chiswick, where the painter resided, he engaging, along with Mrs. Hogarth, to see them properly taken care of. It is impossible to revert to the life of Hogarth, so full of labour in his art, and

at the latter period of his existence, so charged with
vexation and controversy, by reason of the defection
and abuse of his quondam friends, Wilkes and
Churchill, without feeling some degree of admiration
for one, who amidst all this, should be found engaged
in so humble a charity as that of watching over the
destiny of parentless and helpless foundlings.

Charity has the peculiar charm of engaging, for her
attendants, men of all kinds of political sentiments,
but even she is not free from the consequences of
private enmity or animosity. This was evidenced by
the quarrel between Wilkes and Hogarth. They were
both associated in the same work of benevolence at
the Foundling Hospital, meeting at the same board
as Governors, but no sooner did a personal quarrel
arise between them, than they ceased to attend in
their places, as if each was afraid of meeting the
other, even within the walls of Charity herself.

"Before the birth of Hogarth," says Cunningham,
"there are many centuries in which we relied wholly
on foreign skill. With him and after him arose a
succession of eminent painters, who have spread the
fame of British Art far and wide." The works of
some of those who arose with him will be found in
the catalogue of pictures belonging to the Hospital
at the end of this book. Though dazzled by the
luminaries in art of these modern days, we must
not forget that their fires have been kindled by the
lesser lights of the past.

THE CHAPEL.

The Chapel was erected, by subscription, in the year 1747, on the original plan by Mr. Jacobsen, forming the central feature of the north and south fronts of the Hospital building.

Its frontage was then limited in extent to the five middle divisions of the open arcades, and the elevation of the superstructure being detached from the main buildings on each side, presented more distinctness of character in itself, and was advantageous in its effect to the general design of the building. The lower part, or ground plan of the Chapel, was thus isolated by a continued arched corridor, forming a sub-structure for the extension of the upper part, which, on the north and south sides, became a portion of the original building, and was subsequently extended over the east and west ends.

The lower area of the building continues of the original extent, its enclosure forming the appropriate basement of a regular colonnade and entablature of the Ionic order, raised on pedestals, with intermediate continued balustrade, enclosing the front of the sittings in the upper part of the building throughout.

A coved ceiling, of handsome design, springing from the entablature of the colonnade, extends over the central area, or main division of building, with enriched bands and pendants on its soffite, and the ceilings of the side and east-end divisions are enriched by soffites and arched bands, of appropriate unity of design with the architecture of the colonnade.

The west end is entirely appropriated to the occupation of the children, and for the organ and choir.

The design and effect of the interior of this building are admitted to be striking and impressive; and as an instance of the mode of distribution of so large a portion of the congregation, at an upper level, with pleasing uniformity and picturesque architectural effect, without the disfigurement generally attendant upon galleries, under the most favourable circumstances; it may be considered a specimen of some originality, and worthy of observation. Some alteration and improvement of the details of the style and decoration of the interior, was probably made at the period of the extension of this building, and the windows at the eastern end filled with stained glass. This enrichment has lately been extended also to the windows on the south front.

The paneling on the sides of the lower area, forming the basement of the colonnade, being of regular design and suitable proportions for pictures, would, at this favourable period for the advancement of fresco painting, become peculiarly appropriate for a partial, if not entire application of them for sacred subjects, after the great masters, and congenial to the spirit and advancement of the British art, and the distinguished artists that fostered the original establishment of the charity.

The simple and appropriate distinction given to the divisions of paneling immediately connected with the altar-table, on the east side, could always be continued to be maintained. The cost of the erection of the Chapel was £6,490.

Some of the windows of the Chapel are ornamented by the armorial bearings of the governors and benefactors in stained glass, and there is a fine representation of ' Faith, Hope, and Charity,' by Wilmshurst, which forms the centre window of the eastern gallery.

The advertisement inviting subscribers set forth, " that the Governors being earnestly desirous that the children under their care should be early instructed in the principles of religion and morality, and having no place of public worship to which the children and servants of the Hospital could conveniently resort, have resolved to erect a Chapel adjoining to their Hospital; but that no part of the revenue of the said Hospital which is or shall be given for the support of the children, may be diverted from that use; and in order to defray the expense of erecting the said Chapel, they have opened a subscription for that purpose."

His Majesty George II. subscribed £2,000. towards the erection, and afterwards £1,000. towards supplying a preacher in the Chapel, to instruct the children in the Christian religion, and for other incidental expenses. The communion plate was presented by a governor who desired to be " unknown; " and the King's upholsterer gave the velvets for the pulpit, &c.

The Governors had been early taught that their Chapel was capable of being converted into a source of pecuniary means for increasing the usefulness of the work they had in hand. What Handel began, other eminent musicians continued, and the Governors having received several blind children into the establishment (during the general and indiscriminate admission), they were instructed in music, and became a fruitful source of advantage to the funds of the charity. For upwards of one hundred years the Chapel has been established, and if the taste of the public for sacred music has increased, and that taste has any beneficial influence on the minds of the people, it has been one of the humble instruments for effecting it.

The expenses in supporting the Chapel are very considerable, and the only return is from the pew rents and contributions of the public at the Chapel doors.

Should these diminish so as to reduce the income below the expenditure, the Governors would have no alternative but to lessen the attractiveness of the service by dispensing with the choir.

———

Handel.—Handel, as if influenced by a kindred feeling with Hogarth (for genius is ever noble and generous), very soon engaged in the work of charity at this popular institution. On the 4th May, 1749, he attended the committee at the Hospital, and offered a performance of vocal and instrumental music, the money arising therefrom to be applied towards finishing of the Chapel.

This performance is thus alluded to in the " Gentleman's Magazine " of that month :—

" The Prince and Princess of Wales, with a great number of persons of quality and distinction, were at the Chapel of the Foundling Hospital, to hear several pieces of vocal and instrumental music composed by George Frederick Handel, Esq., for the benefit of the foundation. 1st. The music of the late Fire Works, and the anthem on the Peace; 2nd. Select pieces from the oratorio of Solomon, relating to the dedication of the temple; and 3rd. Several pieces composed for the occasion, the words taken from Scripture, applicable to the charity and its benefactors. There was no collection, but the tickets were at half-a-guinea, and the audience above a thousand."

For this act of benevolence on the part of Handel, he was immediately enrolled as one of the Governors and Guardians of the Hospital.

During every year after this, until his infirmity obliged him to relinquish his profession, he superintended personally the performance of his matchless Oratorio of the Messiah, in the Chapel, which netted to the Treasury of the Charity no less a sum than £7,000.

The Governors of the Hospital seeing the profitableness of this performance, and being (as it appeared) misinformed of Handel's intention regarding the copyright, prepared a petition to Parliament to secure it for themselves. The latter part of this petition is as follows:—

"That in order to raise a further sum for the benefit of the said Charity, George Frederick Handel, Esq., hath been charitably pleased to give to this corporation a composition of musick, called 'The Oratorio of the Messiah,' composed by him the said George Frederick Handel, reserving to himself the liberty only of performing the same for his own

L

benefit during his life : and whereas the said benefaction cannot be secured to the sole use of your
petitioners, therefore, humbly pray, that leave may
be given to bring in a bill for the purposes aforesaid."

Upon one of the Governors waiting upon the
musician with this form of petition, he soon discovered
that the committee of the Hospital had built upon
a wrong foundation ; for Handel, bursting into a
rage, exclaimed—" Te Deivel ! for vat sal de Foundling
put mein oratorio in de Parlement ?   Te Deivel !
mein music sal not go to de Parlement ! "

Here the matter dropped, never to be revived.
At the completion of the Chapel, Handel presented
the Governors with an organ, which he opened
on the 1st May, 1750, when the concourse of persons
was so great that the performance was repeated
fifteen days afterwards.   Upon one of these occasions
the audience was conveyed in no less than 800
coaches and chairs.

The Governors of the Hospital felt, naturally
enough, a deep affection and veneration for Handel ;
and therefore, when, in April, 1753, a foolish paragraph
appeared in the daily papers, stating, that he was
preparing a funeral anthem, to be performed in the
Chapel of the Hospital after his death, the Committee
desired their Secretary to acquaint him, " That the
said paragraph has given this Committee great concern,
they being highly sensible that all well-wishers to
this charity must be desirous for the continuance of
his life, who has been and is so great and generous
a benefactor thereto."

With the full concurrence of Handel, the Governors appointed his amanuensis and assistant, Mr. John Christopher Smith, the first organist of the Chapel.

At the death of the great musician, it was found he had made the following bequest:—" I give a fair copy of the score, and all the parts of my oratorio called, 'The Messiah,' to the Foundling Hospital." The Governors resolved, in grateful memory of their friend and benefactor, to have a dirge and funeral anthem performed in the Chapel, on the 26th May, 1759, on the occasion of his demise, which performance took place under the direction of the organist of the Chapel, Mr. John Christopher Smith.

Benjamin West, R.A. — On the finishing of the Chapel, Chevalier Casali presented the Governors with an altar-piece, the subject being "The Offering of the Wise Men." This picture occupied its appropriate place till 1801, when two of the Vice-Presidents, John Wilmot, Esq., and Thomas Everett, Esq., M.P., together with Sir Thomas Bernard, Bart. (the Treasurer), and John Puget, Esq., agreed to purchase and present to the Hospital a picture by West, namely —*Christ presenting a little Child.** This picture had been in the hands of a party, by whose mismangement it had suffered some injury, and therefore West, in

----

* " And Jesus called a little child unto him, and set him in the midst of them,

" And said, Verily I say unto you, Except ye be converted, and become as little children, ye shall not enter into the kingdom of heaven.

" And whoso shall receive one such little child in my name receiveth me."

his determination to make it fully acceptable to the Governors, almost entirely repainted it. " The care" (he says) " with which I have passed that picture, I flatter myself has now placed it in the first class of pictures from my pencil ; at least, I have the satisfaction to find that to be the sentiment of the judges of painting who have seen it."

For this act of generosity, the Governors resolved to elect West one of their corporate body.

He appears to have been highly flattered by this compliment, and in acknowledging it, states that his professional duties will not permit him to become an active member of the Corporation, but to shew his respect and good wishes for the establishment in the only way he could make a return, he intended to add to the embellishments of the Chapel as follows :—

" There are " (he says) " on each side the place of Communion in the Chapel, opposite the Governors' and Governors' Ladies' seats, two panels, well calculated to receive paintings. If the Governors will concur, at my leisure I propose to paint two pictures from sacred history to fill those panels, which I shall beg the Corporation to accept of, as a mark of my respect for the Institution, at the same time, to ask of them the exclusive right of having prints taken from those pictures."

It need not be added that the Governors immediately accepted this munificent and charitable offer, but it is to be lamented that the leisure of the artist never arrived, and that the work remains undone. If perchance any modern artist should read this and have a laudable desire to establish his fame, he cannot do better than carry out the intention of West.

In 1816, the Chapel being then under repair, West had the Altar-Piece taken to his house and again re-touched it, returning it to its place with strong expressions towards this favourite work of his hand.

THE CATACOMBS.

Beneath the Chapel are capacious Vaults, in which were deposited, in 1751, the remains of the Founder, at his own request; since which many of the Governors have also been buried here. The coffins, which are of lead, are enclosed in stone catacombs. Amongst the departed, who were distinguished for their zeal in the cause of the Charity, within whose walls they now rest, the following may be specially noticed, viz. :—

1803.—*The Rev. Samuel Harper, M.A.*
1807.—*William George Sibley, Esq.*
1808.—*Anthony Van Dam, Esq.*
1810.—*Thomas Everett, Esq., M.P.*
1813.—*Michael Heathcote, Esq.*
1818.—*William Watson, Esq., F.R.S.*
1818.—*Sir Thomas Bernard, Baronet.*
1819.—*John Owen Parr, Esq.*
1820.—*William Nanson, Esq.*

1822.—*John Stephenson, Esq.*

1823.—*Robert Raynsford, Esq.*

1827.—*Philip Jackson, Esq.*

1830.—*John Heath, Esq.*

1831.—*Thomas Smith, Esq.*

1831.—*Richard Smith, Esq.*

1832.—*The Right Honourable Lord Tenterden.**

1832.—*William Holden, Esq.*

1834.—*William Hammond, Esq.*

1834.—*Christopher Stanger, M.D*

1838.—*Charles James Johnstone, M.D.*

1839.—*Arthur Browne Blakiston, Esq.*

1839.—*Samuel Compton Cox, Esq.*

1839.—*Sir Stephen Gaselee, Knight.*

1839.—*Hugh Edwards, Esq.*

---

* Lord Tenterden, before the labours of his judicial functions engrossed the whole of his time, took an active part in the administration of the affairs of the Foundling Hospital, and wrote the following verses, to be set to music, and sung at the commemorative festivals of the Governors:—

"The ship sail'd smoothly o'er the sea,
　By gentle breezes fann'd,
When Coram, musing at the helm,
　This happy fabric plann'd:
Not in the schools by sages taught
　To woo fair virtue's form;
But nursed on danger's flinty lap,
　And tutor'd by the storm.

"When threat'ning tempests round him rag'd,
　And swelling billows heav'd,
His bark a wretched orphan seem'd,
　Of aid and hope bereav'd.
If through the clouds a golden gleam
　Broke sweetly from above,
He bless'd the smiling emblem there
　Of charity and love.

1840.—*Anthony V. D. Searle Van Dam, Esq.*
1842.—*Peregrine Dealtry, Esq.*
1844.—*The Rev. John Hewlett, B.D.*
1847.—*Joseph Kay, Esq.*
1849.—*Robert Rainy Pennington, Esq.*
1849—*John Thomas, Esq..*
1850.—*George Pardoe, M.D.*
1852.—*John Mackenzie, Esq.*
1854.—*James Kendle Browne, Esq.*
1855.—*William Hammond, Esq.*
1857.—*Henry Denton, Esq.*

PROPOSAL FOR MAKING THE HOSPITAL AVAILABLE AS A PUBLIC MUSIC SCHOOL.

In July, 1774, Dr. Burney and Mr. Giardini, attended the Court of Governors, and proposed a plan for forming a *Public Music School* by means of

---

" Around the glowing land he spread
  Warm pity's magic spell,
And tender bosoms learn'd from him
  With softer sighs to swell.
Beauty and wealth, and wit and power,
  The various aid combin'd ;
And angels smil'd upon the work
  That Coram had design'd.

" Virtue and meekness mark'd his face
  With characters benign,
And Hogarth's colours yet display
  The lineaments divine ;
Our ground his ashes sanctify,
  Our songs his praise employs ;
His spirit with the bless'd above
  His full reward enjoys."

the children of the Hospital, which, having been taken into consideration, was unanimously accepted as "likely to be of censiderable advantage to this Corporation and of national utility."

The Court immediately set about opening a subscription roll (which received the support of the Dukes of Gloucester and Cumberland), and appointed a special Committee to " digest and form the properest method for carrying the said plan into execution," the Committee to consist of all the members of the Court present, and the Duke of Portland, the Earl of Ashburnham, the Earl of Dartmouth, Lord Le Despencer, and Sir Watkin Williams Wynne, Bart.

But it was the fate of this scheme to be nipt in the bud. Its opponents proposed and carried a resolution at the next Court, which completely set it aside. The resolution was this—" It appeared to this Court that the plan of a public music school by way of employment of the children, is not warranted by the Act of Parliament."

Madame D'Arblay* in her Memoirs of Dr. Burney (her father), gives the following graphical account of this transaction :—

" But neither the pain of his illness, nor the pleasure of his recovery, nor even the loved labours of his history, offered sufficient occupation for the insatiate activity of his mind. No sooner did he breathe again the breath of health, resume his daily business, and return to his nocturnal studies, than a project occurred

---

* The celebrated Miss Burney, author of " Evelina," &c.

to him of a new undertaking, which would have seemed to demand the whole time and undivided attention of almost any other man.

" This was nothing less than to establish, in England, a seminary for the education of musical pupils of both sexes, upon a plan of which the idea should be borrowed, though the execution should almost wholly be new modeled, from the Conservatorios of Naples and Vienna.

"As disappointment blighted this scheme, just as it seemed maturing to fruition, it would be to little purpose to enter minutely into its details; and yet, as it is a striking feature of the fervour of Dr. Burney for the advancement of his art, it is not its failure, through the secret workings of undermining prejudice, that ought to induce his biographer to omit recounting so interesting an intention and attempt; and the less, as a plan, in many respects similar, has recently been put into execution, without any reference to the original projector.

"The motives that suggested this undertaking to Dr. Burney, with the reasons by which they were influenced and supported, were to this effect—

"In England, where more splendid rewards await the favourite votaries of musical excellence than in any other spot on the globe, there was no establishment of any sort for forming such artists as might satisfy the real connoisseur in music; and save English talent from the mortification, and the British purse from the depredations of seeking a constant annual supply of genius and merit from foreign shores.

M

" An institution, therefore, of this character, seemed wanting to the state for national economy, and to the people for national encouragement.

" Such was the enlarged view which Dr. Burney, while yet in Italy, had taken of such a plan for his own country.

" The difficulty of collecting proper subjects to form its members, caused great diversity of opinion and of proposition amongst the advisers with whom Dr. Burney consulted.

" It was peculiarly necessary that these young disciples should be free from every sort of contamination, mental or corporal, upon entering this musical asylum, that they might spread no dangerous contagion of either sort, but be brought up to the practice of the art, with all its delightful powers of pleasing, chastened from their abuse.

" With such a perspective, to take promiscuously the children of the poor, merely where they had an ear for music, or a voice for song, would be running the risk of gathering together a mixed little multitude, which, from intermingling inherent vulgarity, hereditary diseases, or vicious propensities, with the finer qualities requisite for admission, might render the cultivation of their youthful talents, a danger, if not a curse, to the country.

" Yet, the length of time that might be required for selecting little subjects of this unadulterated description from different quarters, with the next to impossibility of tracing, with any certainty, what might have been their real conduct in times past, or what might be their principles to give any basis of security for the time to come, caused a perplexity of the most serious species; for should a single one of the tribe go astray, the popular cry against teaching the arts to the poor would stamp the whole little community with a stain indelible, and the institution itself might be branded with infamy.

"What abstractedly was desirable, was, to try this experiment upon youthful beings to whom the world was utterly unknown, and who, not only in innocence had breathed their infantine lives, but in complete and unsuspicious ignorance of evil.

"Requisites so hard to obtain, and a dilemma so intricate to unravel, led the Doctor to think of the *Foundling Hospital*, in the neighbourhood of which, in Queen Square, stood his present dwelling.

"He communicated, therefore, his project to Sir Charles Whitworth, the Governor of the Hospital. Sir Charles thought it proper, feasible, desirable, and patriotic.

"The Doctor, thus seconded, drew up a plan for forming a musical conservatorio in the metropolis of England, and in the bosom of the *Foundling Hospital*.

"The intention was to collect from the whole little corps all who had musical ears or tuneful voices, to be brought up scientifically as instrumental or vocal performers, Those of the group who gave no decided promise of such qualifications, were to go on with their ordinary education, and to abide by its ordinary result, according to the original regulations of the charity.

"A meeting of the Governors and Directors was convened by their chief, Sir Charles Whitworth, for announcing this scheme. The plan was heard with general approbation, but the discussions to which it gave rise were discursive and perplexing.

"It was objected, that music was an art of luxury, by no means requisite to life, or accessary to morality. These children were all meant to be educated as plain but essential members of the general community. They were to be trained up to useful purposes, with a singleness that would ward off all ambition for what was higher, and teach them to repay the benefit of their support by cheerful labour. To stimulate them to superior views might mar the religious object of the charity, which was to nullify rather than extinguish, all disposition to pride, vice, or voluptuousness, such as, probably, had demoralized their culpable parents, and thrown these deserted outcasts upon the mercy of the *Foundling Hospital*.

"This representation, the Doctor acknowledged, would be unanswerable, if it were decided to be right, and if it were judged to be possible, wholly to extirpate the art of music in the British empire, or, if the *Foundling Hospital* were to be considered as a seminary, predestined to menial servitude, and as the only institution of the country where the members were to form a caste, from whose rules and plodden ways no genius could ever emerge.

"But such a fiat could never be issued by John Bull, nor so flat a stamp be struck upon any portion of his countrymen. John Bull was at once too liberal and too proud to seek to adopt the tame ordinances of the immutable Hindoos, with whom ages passed unmarked, generations unchanged, the poor never richer, the simple never wiser, and with whom, family by family, and trade by trade, begin, continue, and terminate their monotous existence by the same predetermined course, and to the same invariable destiny.

" These children, the Doctor answered, are all orphans; they are taken from no family, for by none are they owned; they are drawn from no calling, for to none are they specifically bred. They are all brought up to menial offices, though they are all instructed in reading and writing, and the females in needlework; but they are all systematically and indiscriminately, destined to be servants or apprentices at the age of fifteen; from which period, all their hold upon the benevolent institution to which they are indebted for their infantine rescue from perishing cold and starving want, with their subsequent maintenance and tuition, is rotarily transferred to new-born claimants ; for the Hospital then has fulfilled its engagements, and the children must go forth to the world, whether to their benefit or their disgrace.

" Were it not better, then, when there are subjects who are success inviting, to bestow upon them professional improvement, with virtuous education? since, as long as operas, concerts, and theatres are licensed by government, musical performers, vocal and instrumental, will inevitably be wanted, employed, and remunerated: and every state is surely best served, and the people of every country are surely the most encouraged, when the nation suffices for itself, and no foreign aid is necessarily called in, to share either the fame or the emoluments of public performances?

" Stop, then ; prohibit, proscribe,—if it be possible —all taste for foreign refinements, and for the exquisite finishing of foreign melody and harmony, or establish a school on our own soil, in which, as in painting and in sculpture, the foreign perfection of arts may be taught, transplanted, and culled, till they become indigenous.

" And where, if not here, may subjects be found on whom such a national trial may be made with the least danger of injury? Subjects who have been brought up with the strictness of regular habits that has warded them from all previous mischief, yet who are too helpless and ignorant, as well as poor, to be able to develope whether or not nature, in her secret workings, has kindled within their unconscious bosoms a spark—a single spark of harmonic fire, that might light them from being hewers of wood and brushers of spiders, to those regions of vocal and instrumental excellence, that might propitiate the project of drawing from our own culture a school for music, of which the students, under proper moral and religious tutelage, might, in time, supersede the foreign auxiliaries by whom they are now utterly extinguished.

" The objectors were charged, also, to weigh well that there was no law or regulation, and no means whatsoever that could prevent any of this little association from becoming singers and players, if they had musical powers, and such should be their wish; though, if self-thrown into that walk, singers and players only at the lowest theatres, or at the tea and public gardens, or even in the streets, as fiddlers of country dances, or as ballad squallers, in which degraded exercise of their untaught endowments, not only decent life must necessarily be abandoned, but immorality, licentiousness, and riot, must assimilate with, or rather form a prominent part of their exhibitions and performances.

"Here the discussion closed. The opponents were silenced, if not convinced, and the trial of the project was decreed. The hardly-fought battle over, victory, waving her gay banners, that wafted to the Doctor hopes of future renown with present benediction, determined him, for the moment, to relinquish even his history, that he might devote every voluntary thought to consolidating this scheme.

"The primary object of his consideration, because the most conscientious, was the preservation of the morals and fair conduct of the pupils. And here, the exemplary character and the purity of the principles of Dr. Burney would have shone forth to national advantage, had the expected prosperity of his design brought his meditated regulations into practice.

"Vain would it be to attempt, and useless, if not vain, to describe his indignant consternation, when, while in the full occupation of these arrangements, a letter arrived to him from Sir Charles Whitworth, to make known, with great regret, that the undertaking was suddenly overthrown. The enemies to the attempt, who had seemed quashed, had merely lurked in ambush, to watch for an unsuspected moment to convene a partial committee, in which they voted out the scheme as an innovation upon the original purpose of the institution ; and pleading, also, an old Act of Parliament against its adoption, they solemnly proscribed it for ever.*

" Yet a repeal of that act had been fully intended, before the plan, which, hitherto, had only been agitating and negotiating, should have been put into execution.

" All of choice, however, and all of respect that remained for Dr. Burney, consisted in a personal offer from Sir Charles Whitworth, to re-assemble an opposing meeting amongst those friends who, previously, had carried the day.

" But happy as the Doctor would have been to have gained, with the honour of general approbation, a point he had elaborately studied to clear from mystifying objections, and to render desirable even to patriotism, his pride was justly hurt by so abrupt a defalcation ; and he would neither with open hostility, nor under any versatile contest, become

---

* This apparent want of liberality on the part of the Governors, in the mental culture of the children, reminds one of a darker period of the history of this small community. Dr. Johnson writes, in 1756 :—" When, a few months ago, I wandered through the Hospital, I found not a child that seemed to have heard of his creed or the commandments. To breed up children in this manner, is to rescue them from an early grave, that they may find employment for the gibbet : from dying in innocence, that they may perish by their crimes."

the founder or chief of so important an enterprise.

" He gave up, therefore, the attempt, without further struggle; simply recommending to the mature reflections of the members of the last Committee, whether it were not more pious, as well as more rational, to endeavour to ameliorate the character and lives of practical musical noviciates, than to behold the nation, in its highest classes, cherish the art, follow it, embellish it with riches, and make it fashion and pleasure; while, to train to that art, with whatever precautions, its appropriate votaries from the bosom of our own country, seemed to call for opposition, and to deserve condemnation.

" Thus died, in its birth, this interesting project, which, but for this brief sketch, might never have been known to have brightened the mind, as one of the projects, or to have mortified it, as one of the failures, of the active and useful life of Dr. Burney."

Happily, the prejudices so fatal to Dr. Burney's scheme, at the period alluded to, do not prevail with the Governors of the present day; whose proceedings, with reference to the same subject, stand out in bold relief, when contrasted with that of their predecessors of 1774,—for when, in 1847, it was demonstrated to them, that the establishment of a *Juvenile Band* of musicians, from amongst the boys, would be attended with advantages to them in life, they did not hesitate readily to adopt the suggestion. The proposal was immediately put into practice, and the results are

N

highly satisfactory, proving (if indeed proof were necessary) that the cultivation of instrumental music amongst the children of the Hospital, *is not attended* with that *degradation of moral character*, so much apprehended in Dr. Burney's time. For not only has the general moral character of those instructed in music been *improved*, their physical capacities enlarged, by the influence of music during their stay in the Hospital; but, as far as has been manifested during the limited time in which music has been taught amongst them, considerable social advantages have been derived by many of them from this source when they have quitted the establishment,— fully demonstrating the practicability of Dr. Burney's scheme, and that there is nothing to fear from the " popular cultivation of music," provided due regard be .had to the scientific treatment of the art.

It is now ten years since the band was formed, numbering about thirty boys from nine to eleven years. This number has, ever since, been maintained, sometimes exceeded. The boys are selected from amongst those who possess a musical ear, due regard being paid to their physical development. As the musical instruments, to which they are placed, are essentially *men's* intruments, considerable physical exertion is required in playing upon them. Great care is, therefore, bestowed in watching the effects this early application produces upon the health of the children ; and no instance has ever occurred of injury being done by blowing. On the contrary, boys of delicate constitution have greatly improved in health from the exercise of a wind instrument.

As a considerable portion of the time allotted to the practice of music is drawn from the ordinary school hours, great care has, also, been taken to ascertain how far the band-boys are—when brought in competition at the annual school examination with other boys not in the band—affected by this arrangement, and the results have shown that a full proportion of the prizes, awarded for scholastic pursuits, has been constantly carried off by band-boys. This success at school may fairly be attributed to the salutary effects of music upon the character of those boys receiving instruction in the art, which imparts a vivacity to their tempers, and, by its enlivening influence, renders the mental capacities more energetic and susceptible of receiving general instruction, than the faculties of the other boys attain, who do not enjoy the advantage of musical tuition.

During the period the band has been formed, about one hundred boys have received instruction, of this number, twenty, at their own desire, have been placed as musicians in the bands of Her Majesty's Household Troops and other regiments, and also in the Royal Navy. Thus, while securing an eligible position in life for the boys, has the formation of the band proved, by saving the expenses of premium and outfit allowed for each boy ordinarily apprenticed, " of considerable advantage to *this corporation and of national utility.*" Nor should it be lost sight of, that very many of the boys who have passed through the band, and are now occupied in various trades to which they have been apprenticed, have followed up their music as a recreation with satisfaction to themselves, and to those with whom it is their lot to be placed.

MEMOIR OF THE FOUNDER.

Captain Coram was born at Lyme Regis, in Dorsetshire, in the year 1668. He was a descendant of the Corhams, of Devonshire; and Kinterbury, in that county, was for several generations, the property and residence of the family.* Of his baptism, there does not appear to be any record at Lyme Regis; and all that can be found in the registers relating to the family is the following:—

"William, son of John Coram, Captain, was baptized at Lyme, April 29th, 1671."†

There seems to be no doubt, therefore, that this "William" was a younger brother of "Thomas," the subject of this memoir, and consequently, that the latter, in devoting himself to the sea service, followed the occupation of his father. At Lyme Regis, which is a sea-port, there was carried on, at the period in question, a considerable coasting

---

* Vide Risdon's Chorographical Description of the County of Devon.
† For this information the writer is indebted to Dr. Hodges, the present Vicar of Lyme Regis.

and Newfoundland trade; and hence we may venture to account for the first direction of his course in maritime concerns.

Of his early years there is no biographical notice extant; but it appears probable, that the ardent temperament which he exhibited through life, was too strong for the restraints of home and domestic ties, and that this, and his love of enterprise, caused him to be, even at the outset of his career, an independent member of his father's family.

About the year 1694 (he being then twenty-six years old), we find him at Taunton, Massachusetts, in the United States, exercising the humble trade of a shipwright. To this new country he had, doubtless, gone in the spirit of adventure; and here he gave the first instance on record of that public devotedness for which he was so remarkable. Whilst in this comparative wilderness, he perceived, with regret, the uncivilized condition of the inhabitants, by reason of the absence of systematic religion, as exercised by by the Church of England of which he was a member. By a deed, therefore, dated 8th December, 1703, he conveyed to the governor and other authorities of Taunton, fifty-nine acres of land. The condition of the gift was this,—that whenever, in the progress of civilization and the increase of population, the people of the place should desire the Church of England to be established there, that then, on their application to the vestrymen, or their successors in office, the land, or a suitable part of it, was to be granted for that purpose, or for a schoolhouse, as they might desire. This gift, the deed alleges, was made "in consideration of the love and respect which the donor had and did bear unto the said church, as also for divers other good causes and considerations him especially at that present moving." In this deed he is described as "of Boston, in New England, sometimes residing in Taunton, in the County of Bristol, Shipwright." At a subsequent period of his life he presented to the parish of Taunton a valuable library, part of which remains to this day. Some of the books appear to have been solicited by Coram from others. Thus, in the copy of Common Prayer now preserved in the church, the entry in the title page is as follows:— "This Book of Common Prayer is given by the Right Honourable Arthur Onslow, Speaker of the Honourable House of Commons of Great Britain, one of His Majesty's Most Honourable Privy Council, and Treasurer of His Majesty's Navy, &c., to *Thomas Coram*, of London, *Gentleman*, for the use of a Church, lately built at Taunton, in New England." Coram appears to have obtained the warm friendship of Mr. Speaker Onslow, of the evidence of which this is not the only instance.

From Taunton Captain Coram removed to Boston, about the close of the seventeenth century, and engaged in commerce. He became a ship-master, and acquired some property in following seas, especially in the then newly-discovered fisheries. By his intercourse with the colonies, at their different ports, he became well acquainted with their wants, and deeply concerned for their welfare; and though in a comparatively humble station, originated many noble plans for their benefit.

In 1704 he was very instrumental in planning and procuring an Act of Parliament, for encouraging the making of Tar in the Northern Colonies of British America, by a bounty to be paid on the importation thereof, whereby not only a livelihood was afforded to thousands of families employed in that branch of trade in North America, but above a million sterling was saved to the nation, which was heretofore obliged to buy all its Tar from Sweden, at a most exhorbitant price, besides being imported in Swedish vessels.

In the year 1719, he was on board the ship " Sea Flower," on her passage to Hamburgh, when she was stranded off Cuxhaven and plundered by the inhabitants of the district of her cargo. Coram, in endeavouring to preserve the property on board, was grossly ill-used by the pirates, who managed to overpower him and the rest of the authorities. In the affidavit relating to this outrage, he is described as " of London, Mariner and Shipwright," and the affidavit further sets forth, " That he (Coram) having usually sold to his Majesty in the year past and at other times, quantities of naval stores from America, for the supply of his Majesty's navy, did about February last, design to visit his Majesty's German dominions to see what supplies of timber and other naval stores could be had from thence, fit for the navy royal." By this incident in the life of Coram, we learn the nature of his transactions at this period, but it would seem that soon afterwards, having accumulated

as much wealth as suited his moderate views, he
retired from the sea service, and devoted himself for
the remainder of his life to projects having for their
object the public good. It was soon after this, that
he turned his attention to the destitute state of the
infant poor of the metropolis, and engaged in
his laudable design of establishing an Hospital for
Foundlings.

Captain Coram was not a mere theorist. All his
schemes were of a practical nature. He first made
himself thoroughly master of his subject, and then
set about convincing those whose assistance he
deemed necessary for their accomplishment. The
difficulty he had to encounter was the want of
that energy of character in others, which was so
remarkable in himself. This retarded the progress
of many of the projects he had set on foot for
the benefit of mankind. The good, however, that
he effected, is sufficiently substantial to hand his
name down to the latest posterity, as the lover of
his country and of her people. The celebrated
Horace Walpole said of him that he was "the
honestest, the most disinterested, and the most
knowing person about the plantations" he ever
talked with. The Colonial concerns of the country
certainly had his special care.

It was at the solicitation of Captain Coram, that
an Act of Parliament was obtained for taking off the
prohibition on importing deal boards and fir timber
from the Netherlands and Germany, on account of
the King of Denmark having enhanced the prices of

those commodities, by which means they immediately fell twenty per cent.

In the year 1732 he was appointed one of the trustees, by a charter from George II. for the settlement of Georgia, in the colonization of which province he took deep interest.

His next project related to Nova Scotia, and about the year 1735 he addressed the following Memorial to George II.*

" *To the King's Most Excellent Majesty in Council.*

" The Memorial of Thomas Coram, Gentleman, most humbly showeth,—

" That your memorialist having, through long experience in naval affairs, and by residing many years in your Majesty's plantations in America, observed, with attention, several matters and things which he conceives might be greatly improved, for the honour and service of the Crown, and the increase of the trade, navigation, and wealth of this kingdom ; he, therefore, most humbly begs leave to represent to your Majesty,—

" That the coasts of your Majesty's province of

---

* There is an honourable testimonial in favour of Captain Coram's character, in a letter from Mr. Horace Walpole, then ambassador at the Hague, to his brother, Sir Robert Walpole, dated the 18th April, 1735 , where, in a colonial matter of considerable importance, which is the subject of the letter, Mr. Walpole closes with these words : " Lose no time in talking with Sir Charles Wager, Mr. Blanden, and one Coram, the honestest, the most disinterested, and the most knowing person about the plantations I ever talked with."

Coxe's Life of Sir Robert Walpole, vol, III., page 243.

Nova Scotia afford the best cod-fishing of any in the known parts of the world, and the land is well adapted for raising hemp, and other naval stores, for the better supplying this kingdom with the same: but the discouragements have hitherto been such as have deterred people from settling there, whereby the said province, for want of good inhabitants, is not so beneficial to this kingdom, nor so well secured to the Crown as it might be; because it cannot be presumed the French inhabitants, who remain there by virtue of the treaty, whereby *Nova Scotia* was surrendered to Great Britain, anno, 1710, being all papist, would be faithful to your Majesty's interest, in case of a war between Great Britain and France.

" Your memorialist, therefore, most humbly conceives that it would be highly conducive to the interests of this kingdom, to settle, without loss of time, a competent number of industrious protestant families in the said province, which is the northern frontier of your Majestys' dominions in America, under a civil government to be established by your Majesty, conformable in all its branches, as near as may be to the constitution of England, which seems the most probable, if not the only means of peopleing this province, which experience shows could not be effected under the military government that hath been exercised there upward of twenty-four years past, and of giving effectual encouragement to the cod-fishery, that valuable branch of British commerce, which hath declined very much of late years, in proportion as the French have advanced therein.

"Your memorialist further begs leave to observe
that the French are masters of the best salt in the
world for curing fish, whereas the English are obliged
to have what salt they use from foreign dominions,
which make it highly necessary to secure a perpetual
supply of salt in your Majesty's dominions in America,
that we may not depend on a precarious supply
of that commodity from the dominions of other
princes.   And your memorialist humbly conceives
that the Island of Exuma, which is one of the
Bahamas, would afford sufficient quantities of salt
for all your Majesty's subjects in North America,
provided Cat Island, another of the Bahamas, lying
to windward of Exuma, was well settled and put in
such a posture, as to be able to cover Exuma and
protect the salt rakers from the depredations of
the Spaniards of Baracoa (the settling of Cat Island
would be otherwise vastly advantageous to the Crown),
and provided the unreasonable demand of the tenth
of all salt raked there be abolished, for want of
which encouragements, the salt ponds of Exuma
have hitherto been useless to the public.

"To these purposes your memorialist humbly lays
the annexed petition at your Majesty's feet, and begs
leave to add that there are several honourable and
worthy persons ready to accept and act in the trust
therein described, if your Majesty shall be pleased
to grant your Royal Letters Patent for that purpose.

"Wherefore he most humbly prays your Majesty
to order that this memorial, together with the
petition hereunto annexed, and whatever your memo-

rialist shall have occasion further to offer, concerning the same, may be taken into consideration, and that your Majesty will be graciously pleased to do therein as your Majesty in your great wisdom and goodness shall seem proper.

"And he will ever pray, &c., &c.

"Thomas Coram."

Accompanying this memorial, was a petition from more than one hundred "labouring handicraftsmen, whose respective trades and callings were overstocked by great numbers of artizans and workmen who resort from all parts of the metropolis, whereby the petitioners were unable to procure sufficient to maintain themselves and families." They further set forth " that to avoid extreme want, and escape the temptations which always attend poverty, they were desirous of being settled securely in some of the plantations of America." The petitioners then state the advantages of the uncultivated tracts of land in the province of Nova Scotia, and pray that they may have the grant of a free passage thither, and when there be protected, their persons and properties by a civil government as near as may be to the constitution of England.

Captain Coram's memorial was referred to the Lords Commissioners for Trade and Plantations, before whom he appeared on several occasions between the years 1735 and 1737, and both verbally and in writing submitted the most satisfactory and elaborate evidence of the propriety and expediency of his proposal, and the laws by which the colony should be maintained and governed, so as to draw the following approval from the Lords Commissioners, addressed to the Privy Council, dated 22nd April, 1737.

" The settlement of Nova Scotia with English inhabitants is of very great consequence to his Majesty's interest in America, and to the interest of this kingdom, from its situation with regard to the French, and from the fishery now carried on at Conso, and the several branches of naval stores that province is capable of producing, when once it shall be settled, as we have several times represented to his Majesty and to your lordships, particularly in our report of the 7th June, 1727; and therefore, we think it very much for his Majesty's service, to give all possible encouragement to any undertaking for this purpose, especially when attended with so great an appearance and probability of success as that of Mr. Coram's, now under our consideration."

Although the object which Captain Coram had in this matter was postponed for several years, owing to political changes and hindrances, yet, before he died, he had the satisfaction of seeing the full development of his plans, in regard to this now valuable colony.

What further relates to this great and good man, and of the different measures which were the objects of his laborious and useful life, cannot be communicated more appropriately than in the language of Dr. Brocklesby, his most intimate friend, who, soon after the death of Coram, thus delineated his character.

"The tribute of praise is due to every virtue—due in proportion to the excellence and extent of that virtue to which it is paid; and consequently, public spirit, which is of all virtues the most conducive to the good of society, deserves as high returns of public gratitude and respect as can possibly be given. This is the rather incumbent on every community where conspicuous instances of this kind appear, because it is indeed the only reward adequate to their merit, and the best method of propagating the example; for what can so properly, or so potently excite public spirit, as the sense of its begetting public love? The most illustrious of all good qualities ought certainly to be honoured with the noblest testimony of affection and esteem.

"There may, indeed, be some kind of restraint, some check upon our zeal during the life of the party, from an apprehension that praise might be mistaken for flattery, and that instead of promoting a general sense of the good man's virtue, it might be the means of exposing him to envy. But when a man is dead, praise is less suspected; and those who would have listened very unwillingly to his commendations when living, will be the first to applaud and support it when he is no more. Whatever prejudices he had to combat, whatever opposition was formed to his designs, while he was busy in the pursuit, the man of public spirit is no sooner at rest from his labours and his life (which always end together), than the sentiments of the public are united on his behalf, and all attend with pleasure to the recital of those actions of the dead, which the living will find difficult to imitate.

"The late Captain Thomas Coram, now gone to his grave in a good old age, with the universal regret of the knowing and upright part of mankind, was a person whose merit and virtues were so extraordinary, exerted with such vigour, and with so great constancy for the benefit of society, that an attempt to raise some little monument to his memory, cannot fail of being well received by the public, whose servant he was for upwards of forty years before his death, without any other wages than the honest satisfaction he felt in doing good and discharging his duty; and will, at the same time, furnish a pleasing employment to one who loved him from the contemplation of his singular character, and for that rugged integrity which distinguished him exceedingly in the present age, and which would have done him no small honour even in better times. An abler hand might have easily undertaken the task, but none could perform it with a better will.

"He was born about the year 1668, bred in the sea-service, and spent the first part of his life in the station of master of a vessel trading to our colonies, by which he gained a perfect acquaintance with that commerce which is of so great consequence, and produces so great profit to this nation. He acquired very early, a sincere and warm attachment to the true interests of his country—had a real concern for them, and did not affect public spirit to cover any private views. His experience was his principal guide, and from thence he learned to consider rational liberty, active industry, and unblemished probity, as the only principles upon which national prosperity could be built; and to these, therefore, he gave his loudest voice and his most earnest endeavours. Free from all hypocrisy, he spoke what he thought with vehemence. But his zeal did not rest in words; it was no less visible in his actions: so that not contented with wishing well to his country, and serving it faithfully in his private and particular capacity, he ventured to step out of the common road, and exerted himself in favour of many projects, from no other motive than their being of general utility.

"It may create some wonder, that without any other qualifications than these, Captain Coram should undertake to form schemes considerable for their extent, and very important in their intentions; and still more wonderful that he should procure, from men of great abilities and long acquaintance with business, an approbation of these schemes, and carry them at length into execution, by dint of unwearied application, and a perseverance that nothing could delay, disturb, or destroy. But this he certainly did, and that without any act but that of disclaiming it— without any address beyond that of showing the advantages which the public would reap from his projects—he actually brought them, sooner or later, to bear, is a position so well supported by facts, that, though it is a little improbable, it must be believed.

" But if he wanted certain accomplishments—if he was deficient in some things which are thought necessary to form a successful solicitor, he had certain talents that supplied these defects. He had an honesty that, though it was a little rough, carried such apparent marks of its being genuine, that those who conversed with him but a little, lost all apprehensions of being deceived; and if this did not give him an easier entrance, it certainly procured him an earlier confidence than would have resulted from a more polished behaviour. His arguments were nervous, though not nice — founded commonly upon facts, and the consequences that he drew, so closely connected with them, as to need no further proof than a fair explanation. When once he made an impression, he took care it should not wear out; for he enforced it continually by the most pathetic remonstrances. In short, his logic was plain sense, his eloquence, the natural language of the heart.

" When the possession of Nova Scotia was first recovered to the crown of Great Britain by force of arms, and secured afterwards by a treaty of peace, Captain Coram very early saw the consequence that this province was of to the natural interest of this nation and her colonies. He was, therefore, very eager and very earnest to have it thoroughly settled, which, if once done, he very well knew, that the advantages arising from agriculture, fishing, and trade, for which, from the richness of its soil, the convenience of its coasts, and the multiplicity of its harbours, it was admirably

P

adapted, would make the value of it quickly known. In this, if he had not the good fortune which he expected and deserved, he was totally disappointed; and, at the same time, had the pleasure to perceive, that the more his notions were attended to, and the closer they were examined, the plainer and more probable they appeared; so that the utility of his scheme was acknowledged in a much greater degree than was, at that time of day, held expedient to carry it into execution.

"But as plans for the public service, well laid, though they sleep for a long time, seldom fail of waking at last, when, through a train of unlooked-for accidents and unexpected events, administrations are roused to attention, so, before his death, he had the satisfaction of seeing his old scheme revived, and this province, which had been so long neglected, owned and considered in that light in which he had long before placed it. This must certainly have given him great consolation, more especially when he perceived that it was carried on under the auspice of a noble person nearly allied to him in sentiment, and who had no other motive to that care and concern which he has shown for this rising colony but his affection to his country, and to whatever may contribute to strengthen her extensive empire, and secure the continuance of that prosperity which she derives from naval power, and settlements well placed and worthily directed.

"May such noble attempts meet with that success they deserve! May this country, so well situated, be thoroughly peopled and effectually cultivated! May protestants from every climate meet therein with a happy retreat from all kinds of oppression, and, by the help of their own industry, under the protection of the British Government, acquire a comfortable assistance, which they will never want spirit to defend!

"He was highly instrumental in promoting another good design—a design equally beneficial to Britain at home, and British subjects abroad, which coalition of interests is a thing always to be wished, and may, as in this case actually it was, be without much difficulty accomplished. The design here intended was the procuring a bounty upon naval stores imported from the colonies—a matter of vast advantage to the mother country, as it freed her from the necessity of dependence upon foreigners for commodities of essential consequence to her strength, and even to her safety, as it prevented the purchasing them with ready money, which was, in effect, saving so much treasure, and, as it exempted her from many difficulties which she had often felt, and from the apprehension of which she could not otherwise be delivered—points, one would imagine, of so serious a nature, as, if once proposed, to command the strictest attention, and the truth of which, once known, from a close examination, never to be let slip out of memory. The design was likewise of infinite benefit to the colonies, because it afforded the means of enriching them by returns from Britain, which, though nature furnished them with the commodities they could not otherwise have had. It removed impediments that had long subsisted

—it opened a way for improvement, that, though often wished for, could not but with the assistance of this method be attempted ; and it converted into value and use, lands and timber that would otherwise have produced nothing. To the inhabitants of the colonies, therefore, there could be nothing more satisfactory—hardly anything so advantageous. But though this is saying a great deal, yet it is not all.

"As salutary and as profitable as this measure might be, considered in these distinct lights, yet its worth was heightened, its importance raised, and its utility demonstrated from another consideration, which was, its uniting the mother country and her daughters in those points of interest which ought to be eminently dear to both. At the same time that it freed Great Britain from depending upon foreigners, it made her sensibly feel the support she received from her plantations ; and while the colonies reaped a just return of profit from this assistance, they were, at the same time more closely connected, and taught to discover the strong and inseparable ties by which they were bound to the mother country. These were the undeniable consequences of Captain Coram's project, and which will do eternal honour to his memory : they were the true and only motives to that ardour with which he pursued it. Enthusiasm was natural to his constitution ; but it was a political enthusiasm of the most noble kind—it was that of laying out all his faculties for the public good.

"But we must not imagine that this gentleman's knowledge of and love for the colonies carried him, in any degree, out of that path which a true Briton ought to tread. He loved the daughters dearly; but he loved them as daughters, and therefore could not brook the least disrespect or disobedience in them towards their parent. The hatters, a very industrious and a very useful body of our manufacturers, thought themselves, with reason, aggrieved by the method taken, in some of the plantations, to interfere with their trade at foreign markets. Captain Coram no sooner heard of this complaint, than he examined it attentively and impartially, and when he perceived that it was founded in right, he espoused it with spirit, he prosecuted it with diligence, and he obtained for that laborious and indefatigable people all the redress they could expect. They would have acknowledged this service by a grateful and handsome return; but Captain Coram had a notion, that if a man's hands were not empty, they could not long be clean: he had a just sense of their gratitude, but did not care to have it expressed by any other present than that of a hat, which he received as often as he had occasion, and, which, in its size, spoke the good wishes of the makers in a very legible character.

"In his private life, this gentleman showed the same probity, the same cheerfulness, the same frankness, the same warmth, and the same affection that he discovered in matters which respected the public; so that, as a master and as a husband, he acted upon the same principles that he would have certainly shown if he had been raised to any conspicuous station of life. It is necessary to mention this, that the uniformity of his conduct may appear, which is the truest method of judging of men's real characters, so as to leave no scruple or doubt upon the minds even of the most cautious enquirers. Beheld in this light, there could not well be conceived a man of greater simplicity of manners. What he thought, he spoke; what he wished, he declared without hesitation, pursued without relaxation or disguise, and never considered obstacles any farther than to discover means to surmount them.

"While he lived in that part of this metropolis which is the common residence of seafaring people, he used to come early into the city, and return late, according as his business required his presence; and both these circumstances afforded him frequent occasions of seeing young children exposed, sometimes alive, sometimes dead, and sometimes dying, which affected him extremely. The reader cannot wonder at this; for a public-spirited man is always humane: and he who is inclined to wear out his life in rendering services to his fellow-subjects, will naturally have the most tender feeling for the sufferings of his fellow-creatures. This was precisely Mr. Coram's case: he saw this calamity in its proper light, and, like an honest and worthy man, thought it would do honour to the nation to show a public spirit of compassion for children thus deserted, through the indigence or cruelty of their parents, and the rather because this was already done in other countries.

"He began, in respect to this design, as he did in all others, with making it the topic of his conversation, that he might learn the sentiments of other men, and from thence form some notion whether what he had in view was practicable. It was not long before he concluded in the affirmative, and, upon frequent trials, he found that there were numbers of all ranks of his sentiments, and not a few who thought it a shame, that a charity so obvious, so useful, and so necessary, should have been so long neglected. This pleased him extremely, and he undertook, with the greatest alacrity possible, to bring so noble, so beneficent, so charitable, so national, and so christian an undertaking to bear, by procuring for it the sanction of public authority. But, alas! he found his expectations strangely disappointed by an infinity of cross accidents that would certainly have wearied out the patience of a man whose resolution had not been equal to the vehemence of his temper. To this circumstance Mr. Coram opposed an unrelenting perseverance, arising from a well-founded persuasion, that if the design was not carried into execution by him, it might for a long time, perhaps for ever, remain abortive.

"This laudable, this invincible obstinacy, carried him through seventeen years of labour, which scarce any other man would have supported for seventeen months, if his own private fortune had been the basis of his pursuit. In this space, the opinion of the public had been frequently declared on his side; and several persons of sound sense and enlarged minds actually bequeathed considerable sums to this charity, when it should have a legal authority, which was the highest testimony they could possibly bear of their sense of its utility. Our advocate for the helpless and the unborn left no stone unturned, let no opportunity slip, but continued to solicit where he had no interest, with as much ardour and anxiety as if every deserted child had been his own, and the cause of the unfounded Hospital that of his family. His arguments moved some—the natural humanity of the own temper more—his firm and generous example most of all; and even people of rank began to be ashamed to see a mans hair become grey in the course of a solicitation by which he was to get nothing. Those who did not enter far enough into the case to compassionate the unhappy infants for whom he was a suitor, could not help pitying him, or indeed forbear admiring a virtue so much more worthy of respect, considering the age in which it was exerted—a virtue which would have done honour to the most virtuous nations in the most virtuous periods—a virtue that made an impression even on such as thought it incomprehensible. But however it was, an impression it made, and a general disposition appeared in favour of this charity. It is, however, doubtful what effect this would have had, or how soon that effect might have been produced, if it had any.

"But this good man, whose head was fertile in expedients, bethought himself at last of applying to the ladies. He knew their nature, he knew their influence, and soon found that he was in the right road. They did not listen much to his arguments,

for the sweetness of their own tempers supplied
a tenderness that rendered arguments unnecessary.
They concurred with Mr. Coram in his design, and
they concurred in his own way. They were earnest,
assiduous, and sincere, and manifested a greater
eagerness to do good than the most self-interested
dare avow in pursuits upon their own account. This
answered its end; and, by the help of these auxiliaries,
Mr. Coram was enabled to procure a charter, to
prevent the most infamous of all murders, because
the most unnatural, and which will supply thousands
of useful subjects to the crown of Great Britain—
a charter which did honour to the great seal, and
spoke, in a literal sense, that prince whose stamp it
bore—the father of his people, as he was before
confessed in every other sense whatever.

" On Tuesday, November 20th, 1739, was held at
Somerset House, the first general meeting of the
nobility and gentry, appointed by his Majesty's Royal
charter to be Governors and Guardians of the Hospital
for the maintenance and education of exposed and
deserted young children, to hear their charter read,
and to appoint their Secretary and a Committee.
Previous to the reading of the charter, Captain
Coram, the petitioner for the charter, addressed his
Grace the Duke of Bedford, the President, in the
following manner:—

" ' My Lord Duke of Bedford,
' It is with inexpressible pleasure I now present
your Grace, at the head of this noble and honourable

Q

corporation, with his Majesty's royal charter, for establishing an Hospital for exposed children, free of all expense, through the assistance of some compassionate great ladies, and other good persons.

'I can, my lord, sincerely aver, that nothing would have induced me to embark in a design so full of difficulties and discouragements, but a zeal for the service of his Majesty, in preserving the lives of great numbers of his innocent subjects.

'The long and melancholy experience of this nation has too demonstrably shewn, with what barbarity tender infants have been exposed and destroyed, *for want of proper means of preventing the disgrace, and succouring the necessities of their parents.*

'The charter will disclose the extensive nature and end of this Charity, in much stronger terms than I can possibly pretend to describe them, so that I have only to thank your Grace and many other noble personages, for all that favourable protection which hath given life and spirit to my endeavours.

'My Lord, although my declining years will not permit me to hope seeing the full accomplishment of my wishes, yet I can now rest satisfied, and it is what I esteem an ample reward of more than seventeen years expensive labour and steady application, that I see your Grace at the head of this charitable trust, assisted by so many noble and honourable Governors.

'Under such powerful influences and directions, I am confident of the final success of my endeavours, and that the public will one day reap the happy and lasting fruits of your Grace's and this Corporation's measures, and as long as my life and poor abilities endure, I shall not abate of my zealous wishes and most active services for the good and prosperity of this truly noble and honourable Corporation.' "

" After the charter was read, Dr. Mead, in the most pathetic manner, set forth the necessity of such an Hospital, and the vast advantages that must accrue to the nation by this useful establishment, which was received with universal approbation, because nobody could entertain the least doubt of the truth or certainty of what the Doctor said.

"At a subsequent Court, the same learned person moved, that the thanks of the Corporation might be given to Mr. Thomas Coram, for his indefatigable and successful applications in favour of this charity, which otherwise would have wanted a legal foundation. It may be easily supposed, that the good old man was not insensible on receiving the only reward of which his labours were capable. But he was just, as well as generous, and would not take more to himself than he deserved. He therefore desired that the thanks of the Corporation might be likewise given to the ladies,* through whose assistance his own endeavours

---

* Even in the case of the "ladies" he had sometimes to encounter difficulties. Attached to a memorial addressed "To H. R. H. the Princess Amelia," now lodged at the Hospital, is the following note :—

"On Innocent's Day, the 28th of December, 1737, I went to St. James's Palace to present this petition, having been advised first to address the lady of the bed-chamber in waiting to introduce it. But the Lady Isabella Finch, who was the lady in waiting, gave me very rough words, and bid me gone with my petition, which I did, without opportunity of presenting it."

became effectual, and he was accordingly empowered to return them the thanks of that honourable body, which was an additional pleasure to a mind sincere and grateful like his.

"Time and accidents could make but little alteration in his temper. The motives from which he first espoused this charity, kept him always attached to its interests; he often visited the Hospital, and saw the children rescued from misery by his care and compassion, with as much pleasure and tenderness as if they had been his own, as indeed in some sense they were. He beheld the lists of benefactors with more pleasure than a miser regards those of his securities. He had the same delight in perceiving the quick progress of this excellent establishment, as a man of another turn would have felt from the improvement of his own estate. This was peculiar to his character —this was the ruling passion of his mind—this was the elixir that kept him from feeling the frowns of fortune in the winter of his age. Wrapt in that cloak of public spirit, which, though worn for so many years, never grew threadbare, he heard those storms whistle around him, unmoved, which would have frighted a person of ordinary courage out of his wits.

"For the truth is, honest reader, and I must not conceal it, that this worthy man, who could feel so much for others, felt but little for himself. After he lost his wife, the only loss for which he ever showed much regret, he was so attentive to public affairs, as to be a little too careless of his own, insomuch, that he might have known even this evil, which no man could

have known, while it was in his power to relieve.
But his friend Mr. Gideon, who loved him for loving
the public, interposed, and obtained a subscription for
his comfortable support, towards which, His Royal
Highness the late Prince of Wales subscribed twenty
guineas per annum, and paid it with as much punctuality
as any of the rest of the subscribers, who were most
of them merchants; and upon this friendly assistance
which he lived to want, but not to ask, he subsisted
for some time, which gave him an opportunity to form
new schemes of the same kind with those he had
executed already; schemes full of goodness, and
which had a tendency to spread the influence of Britain,
and to expand the nation's glory in the like degree.

"The reader may be surprised—and indeed his
surprise will be very excusable—that a person whose
worth and services were so well known should be
left to such distress, and that in a country where the
public pays so much to place-men, no notice should
be taken of a man who deserved a place so well as
Mr. Coram did. But first of all, it must be considered,
that though the public discharge the expense of many,
yet their choice is asked in filling very few places.
Our hero had, indeed, very great qualities, but they
were far from being well turned for anything of this
kind. He who had spent his life in soliciting for
others, could not speak a word for himself. It is,
therefore, no wonder that he was not provided for.
Dumb men are not fit for places. But if the reader
enquires why he did not speak, the answer may not
be difficult. Men of true public spirit are, of all

others, the most ashamed to ask private favours. In others it would be pride, in them it is the effect of principle. It may be said, then, a place should have been given him. To this there can be no reply ; yet, perhaps, it may be some excuse to say, that, while a multitude of claims are put in for every place, we have no reason to be amazed, that a man who would never ask should always be forgot.

"But Providence provided for him, and he had a comfortable subsistence to the last, by a method that he did not, nor indeed could take amiss. He was maintained by the voluntary subscription* of men of public spirit : this was an honour to them, and an honour to him. Had his distress been generally known, he might, no doubt, have been more amply provided for; but this was what he did not want, and what he would never seek. He was content with a little—pleased with being his own master, and with having the liberty to employ his thoughts, to the end of his life, in the same manner that they had been employed from the beginning—in contriving for the public benefit; for whatever his circumstances were, his heart could never be narrow.

---

* On Dr. Brocklesby applying to Captain Coram, to know whether a subscription being opened for his benefit would not offend him, he received this noble answer :—" I have not wasted the little wealth of which I was formerly possessed in self-indulgence and vain expenses, and am not ashamed to confess that, in this my old age, I am poor."

Upon the death of Coram, this pension was continued to poor old Leveridge, for whose volume of songs Hogarth had, in 1727, engraved a title-page and frontispiece, and who, at the age of ninety, had scarcely any other prospect than that of a parish subsistence.—*John Ireland.*

" His last design, now left an orphan to the public care, which it well deserves, was a scheme for uniting the Indians in North America more closely to the British interest, by an establishment for the education of Indian girls. This is, indeed, a very political contrivance ; for if the girls be brought up in Christian principles, we have just grounds to hope—indeed, we have no reason to doubt—that the Indian children, of both sexes, in the next generation, will be brought up Christians. This would be a refined stroke of policy ; for he is the wisest and ablest of all politicians who, by promoting the glory of God, interests the Divine Providence in extending the power of any nation. We know in how wonderful a manner the gospel was propagated ; and we may confidently expect, that when this is sincerely the aim of any government, the same assistance will not be wanting : for whatever men may do, the great Author of all things never alters his maxims, and to follow them is the most infallible method of securing, might we not say commanding, success. May this charitable and pious purpose, in which he lived long enough to make some progress, be completed in virtue of his proposal ; and let the benighted Indians in America join with the deserted Foundlings in Britain in blessing the memory of this worthy man, by which a provision was made that they should come to the knowledge of truth, and of the means of making themselves happy here by their industry, and by their piety, hereafter.

" If it had been in our power to have taken notice of all the other instances he gave of beneficence,

fortitude, and love for society, which are the true
virtues of a patriot, this little work would swell to
a volume. What is here said, therefore, must be
regarded as an imperfect and hasty sketch of his
character, which however may, from its intention,
rather than performance, be agreeable to his friends,
and may perhaps serve, in some. measure, to excite
in others a desire of imitating so amiable an example;
for who that has any respect for virtue, any appetite
to laudable and spotless fame—the noblest purchase
that human industry can make—can be insensible to
that just and general concern which the best and
worthiest men in this metropolis have shown for the
loss of Captain Coram, or that readiness with which
they have expressed their approbation of his conduct,
and the voluntary testimonies they have given to
his merit and services. These are things that will
affect those who are above the common pursuits of
the world, who seek not either tinsel grandeur or the
embarrassment of riches, but yet are far from leading
a life of indolence, or disclaiming all pretensions to
that glory which is so properly the reward of virtue,
that it can attend on nothing else.

"This singular and memorable man exchanged
this life for a better, and passed from doing to
enjoying good, on Friday, March 29th, 1751, in the
four-score and fourth year of his age, making it his
last request, that his corpse might be interred in
the Chapel of the Foundling Hospital, which shows
he had that excellent foundation at his heart, when
all things that regarded this world besides were out

of his thoughts—a circumstance that demonstrates the steadiness of his *affection, and the happiness he had of what he had done for this place, when he was on the point of going where pious and charitable actions afford the highest recommendations —where his merit in that and other respects will be fully known and fully rewarded.

"Accordingly, on Wednesday, the 3rd of April, agreeable to his request, his remains were interred in the Chapel of this Hospital, his pall supported by six, and his funeral attended by a great number of the honourable and worthy persons who are Governors of this useful charity, and who manifested, upon this melancholy occasion, that sincere regard for the deceased, and the pleasure they took 'in paying this deserved respect to his memory—a ceremony which, joined to the high reputation and numerous acquaintance of the deceased, could not have failed of attracting abundance of public-spirited persons, desirous of giving this last mark of their esteem for a man of Mr. Coram's worth, and who, through the progress of a long life, had shown himself a laudable as well as active member of society.

"But the concourse was much increased, and the solemnity of the funeral greatly heightened, by the voluntary appearance of the choir of St. Paul's Cathedral, who were at the Hospital, ready in their surplices to receive the body, and who performed, with the universal approbation of a crowded and distinguished audience, a grave and noble piece of music, suitable to the sad occasion, and which, with

R

the genuine testimonies of sorrow, not to be suppressed, did all the honour to this good man that even the piety and affection of his friends could expect. The Governors of the Hospital have it also in their intention to raise a suitable monument, though, indeed, the Hospital itself may be so styled, that posterity may be the better acquainted with his virtues, and their gratitude.

"Let me be permitted to conclude, with what may add some degree of merit to this little piece, deficient enough in other respects, the words made use of by a friend of his, in the paragraph which gave the first hint to this performance, and which is, indeed, a true character of Mr. Thomas Coram in very few words :—

"'*That when others are remembered by titles and adulations, his shall be nobler fame to have lived above the fear of everything but an unworthy action.*'"

The following Inscription, cut in stone, is placed in the southern arcade of the Chapel.

" CAPTAIN THOMAS CORAM,

whose name will never want a monument
so long as this Hospital shall subsist,
was born in the year 1668 ;
a man eminent in the most eminent virtue,
the love of mankind ;
little attentive to his private fortune,
and refusing many opportunities of increasing it,
his time and thoughts were continually employed
in endeavours to promote the public happiness,
both in this kingdom and elsewhere ;
particularly in the Colonies of North America ;

and his endeavours were many times crowned
with the desired success.
His unwearied solicitation, for above seventeen years together
(which would have baffled the patience and industry
of any man less zealous in doing good),
and his application to persons of distinction, of both sexes,
obtained at length the Charter of the Incorporation
(bearing date the 17th of October, 1739),
for the maintenance and education
of exposed and deserted young children,
by which many thousands of lives
may be preserved to the public, and employed in a frugal
and honest course of industry.
He died the 29th March, 1751, in the 84th of his age ;
poor in worldly estate, rich in good works :
and was buried, at his own desire, in the Vault underneath this
Chapel (the first there deposited) at the east end thereof,
many of the governors and other gentlemen
attending the funeral to do honour to his memory.

Reader,

Thy actions will show whether thou art sincere
in the praises thou may'st bestow on him ;
and if thou hast virtue enough to commend his virtues,
forget not to add also the intimation of them."

There has, also, recently been placed in front of the Hospital a fine Statue of the Founder,

By WILLIAM CALDER MARSHALL, Esq., R.A.

CATALOGUE OF PICTURES, &c.

AT THE

FOUNDLING HOSPITAL.

HAGAR AND ISHMAEL.

"*And the angel of the Lord called to Hagar out of heaven, and said to her, What aileth thee, Hagar? Fear not; for God hath heard the voice of the lad where he is.*"

BY HIGHMORE.

LITTLE CHILDREN BROUGHT TO CHRIST.

"*Jesus said, Suffer little children to come unto me, and forbid them not: for of such is the kingdom of heaven.*"

BY JAMES WILLS.

THE FINDING OF THE INFANT MOSES IN THE BULL-RUSHES.

"*And the maid went and called the child's mother. And Pharoah's daughter said unto her, Take this child and nurse it up for me, and I will give thee thy wages.*"

BY FRANCIS HAYMAN, R.A.

MOSES BROUGHT TO PHAROAH'S DAUGHTER.

" And the child grew, and she brought him unto Pharoah's daughter, and he became her son. And she called his name Moses."

By HOGARTH.

" The subject of this picture," says Nichols, " is taken at the point of time when the child's mother, whom the princess considers as merely its nurse, has brought him to his patroness, and is receiving from the treasurer the wages of her services.

" The little foundling naturally clings to his nurse though invited to leave her by the daughter of a monarch ; and the eyes of an attendant and a whispering Ethiopian, convey an oblique suspicion that the child has a nearer affinity to their mistress than she chooses to acknowledge."

On each side of these large pictures are smaller ones, of a circular form, representing the principal Hospitals of the day, viz.:—

GREENWICH HOSPITAL. — CHRIST'S HOSPITAL. — ST. THOMAS'S HOSPITAL.

By SAMUEL WALE, R.A.

CHELSEA AND BETHLEHEM HOSPITALS.

By HAYTLEY.

A SKETCH OF THE CHARTERHOUSE.
By THOMAS GAINSBOROUGH, R.A.

ST. GEORGE'S HOSPITAL, AND FOUNDLING HOSPITAL.
By RICHARD WILSON, R.A.

Over the Mantle-piece of the Court-room is a beautiful basso-relievo,

By RYSBRACK,

representing children engaged in navigation and husbandry, being the employments to which the children of the Hospital were supposed to be destined.

The side table, of Grecian marble, is supported by carved figures in wood, representing children playing with a goat, and was presented by Mr. John Sanderson (architect), who was employed with others in the erection of the Hospital.

There are also two fine busts, in the Court-room, casts from the Antique, one of Caracalla and the other of Marcus Aurelius. They were given by Mr. Richard Dalton, who held several important offices connected with the arts, and was sent to Italy by George III. to collect articles of *vertu* to enrich His Majesty's collection.

The ornamented ceiling was done by Mr. Wilton, the father of the eminent sculptor.

THE MARCH TO FINCHLEY.

By HOGARTH.

The following is considered the most authentic account of this celebrated picture, and is from the pen of Mr. Justice Welsh, the intimate friend and companion of Hogarth.

"The scene of this representation is laid at Tottenham Court Turnpike; the King's Head, Adam and Eve, and the turnpike house, in full view; beyond which are discovered, parties of the guards, baggage, &c., marching towards Highgate, and a beautiful distant prospect of the country; the sky finely painted. The picture, considered together, affords a view of a military march, and the humours and disorders consequent thereon. Near the centre of the picture, the painter has exhibited his principal figure, which is a handsome young grenadier, in whose face is strongly depicted repentance mixed with pity and concern; the occasion of which is disclosed by two females putting in their claim for his person, one of whom has hold of his right arm, and the other has *seized* his left. The figure upon his right hand, and perhaps placed there by the painter by way of preference, as the object of love is more desirable than that of duty, is a fine young girl in her person, debauched, with child, and reduced to the miserable employ of selling ballads, and who, with a look full of love, tenderness, and distress, casts up her eyes upon her undoer, and with tears descending down her cheeks, seems to say,

'sure you cannot—will not leave me!' The person
and deportment of this figure well justifies the painter's
turning the body of the youth towards her. The
woman upon the left is a strong contrast to this
girl; for rage and jealousy have thrown the human
countenance into no amiable or desirable form. This
is the wife of the youth, who, finding him engaged
with such an *ugly slut*, assaults him with a violence
natural to a woman whose person and beauty are
neglected. Added to the fury of her countenance,
and the dreadful weapon her tongue, another terror
appears in her hand, equally formidable, which is a
roll of papers, whereon is written 'The Remembrancer;'
a word of dire and triple import; for while it shows
the occupation the *amiable bearer* is engaged in, it
reminds the youth of an unfortunate circumstance
he would gladly forget; and the same word is also a
cant expression to signify the blow she is meditating.
And here, I value myself upon hitting the true
meaning, and entering into the spirit of the great
author of that celebrated Journal, called 'The
Remembrancer.'

"It is easily discernible that the two females are
of different parties. The ballad of 'God save our
noble King,' and a print of 'the Duke of Cumberland,'
in the basket of the girl, and the cross upon the
back of the wife, with the implements of her occupation,
sufficiently denote the painter's intention; and what
is truly beautiful, these incidents are applicable to the
march. The hard-favoured sergeant directly behind,
who enjoys the foregoing scene, is not only a good

contrast to the youth, but also, with other helps, throws forward the principle figure. Upon the right of the grenadier is a drummer, who also has his *two remembrancers*, a woman and a boy, the produce of their kinder hours; and who have laid their claim by a violent seizure upon his person. The figure of the woman is that of a complainant, who reminds him of her great application, as well in sending him clean to guard, as other kind offices done, and his promises to make her an honest woman, which he, base and ungrateful, has forgot, and pays her affection with neglect. The craning of her neck shows her remonstrances to be of the shrill kind, in which she is aided by the howling of her boy. The drummer, who has a mixture of fun and wickedness in his face, having heard as many reproaches as suit his present inclination, with a bite of his lip and a leering eye, applies to the instrument of noise in his profession, and endeavours to drown the united clamour, in which he is luckily aided by the *ear-piercing fife* near him.

" Between the figures before described, but more back in the picture, appears the important but meagre phiz of a Frenchman, in close whisper with an Independent. The first I suppose a spy upon the motion of the army ; the other probably drawn into the crowd, in order to give intelligence to his brethren, at their next meeting, to commemorate their noble struggle in support of independence. The Frenchman exhibits a letter, which he assures him contains positive intelligence that ten thousand of his countrymen are landed in England in support of liberty and independence. The joy with which his friend receives these glorious tidings, causes him to forget the wounds upon his head, which he has unluckily received by a too free and premature declaration of his principles. There is a fine contrast in the smile of innocence in the child at the woman's back, compared with the grim joy of a gentleman by it; while the hard countenance of its mother gives a delicacy to the grenadier's girl. Directly behind the drummer's *quondam* spouse, a soldier is reclining against a shed, near which is posted a quack-bill of Dr. Rock; and directly over him a wench at a wicket is archly taking a view, both of the soldier and of the march. Behind the drummer, under the sign of the Adam and Eve, are a group of figures, two of which are engaged in the fashionable art of bruising; their equal dexterity is shown by *sewed-up peepers* on one side, and *a pate well sconced* on the other. And here the painter has shown his impartiality to the merit of our *youths* (who, their minds inflamed with a love of glory, appear, not only encouragers of this truly laudable science, but many of them are also great proficients in the art itself), by introducing a youth of quality, whose face is expressive of those boisterous passions necessary to form a hero of this kind; and who, entering deep into the scene, endeavours to inspire the combatants with a noble contempt of bruises and broken bones. An old woman, moved by a foolish compassion, endeavours to force through the crowd, and part the fray, in which design she is stopped by a fellow who prefers fun and mischief to humanity. Above their heads appears *Jackey James*, a cobbler, a little man of meagre frame, but full of spirits, who enjoys the combat, and with fists clenched, in imagination deals blow for blow with the heroes. This figure is finely contrasted by a heavy, sluggish fellow just behind. The painter, with a stroke of humour peculiar to himself, has exhibited a figure shrinking under the load of a heavy box upon his back, who, preferring curiosity to ease, is a spectator, and waits, in this uneasy state, the issue of the combat. Upon a board next the sign, where roots, flowers, &c., were said to be sold, the painter has humourously altered the words *Tottenham Court Nursery*, alluding to a bruising booth then in that place, and the group of figures underneath.

" Passing through the turnpike, appears a carriage laden with the implements of war, as drums, halberds, tent-poles and hoop-petticoats. Upon the carriage are two old women-campaigners, funking their pipes, and holding a conversation, as usual, in fire and smoke. The grotesque figures afford a fine contrast to a delicate woman upon the same carriage, who is suckling a child. This excellent figure evidently proves, that the painter is as capable of succeeding in the graceful style as in the humourous. A little boy lies at the feet of this figure ; and the painter, to show him of martial breed, has placed a small trumpet in his mouth.

" The serious group of the principal figures in the centre is finely relieved by a scene of humour on the

left. Here an officer has seized a milk wench, and
is rudely kissing her. While the officer's ruffles
suffer in this action, the girl pays her price, by an
arch soldier, who, in her absence of attention to her
pails, is filling his hat with milk, and, by his
waggish eye, seems also to partake in the kissing
scene. A chimney-sweeper's boy, with glee, puts in
a request to the soldier, to supply him with a cap
full when his own turn is served; while another
soldier points out the fun to a fellow selling pies,
who, with an inimitable face of simple joy, neglects
the care of his goods, which the soldier dexterously
removes with his other hand. In the figure of the
pieman the pencil has exceeded all power of description. The old soldier, divested of one spatterdash,
and near losing the other, is knocked down by all-
potent gin: upon calling for *t'other cogue*, his waggish
comrade, supporting him with one hand, endeavours
to pour water into his mouth with the other, which
the experienced old one rejects with disdain, puts
up his hand to his wife, who bears the arms and
gin-bottle, and who, well acquainted with his taste,
is filling a quartern. Here the painter exhibits a
sermon upon the excessive use of spirituous liquors,
and the destructive consequences attending it; for
the soldier is not only rendered incapable of his
duty, but (what is shocking to behold) a child, with
an emaciated countenance, extends its little arms
with great earnestness, and wishes for that liquor
of which it seems well acquainted with the taste.
And here, not to dwell wholly upon the beauties

of this painting, I must mention an absurdity discovered by a professed connoisseur in painting. ' Can there,' says he ' be a greater absurdity than the introducing a couple of chickens so near a crowd? And not only so; but see!—their direction is to go to objects it is natural for them to shun. Is this knowledge of nature? Absurd to the last degree!' And here, with an air of triumph, ended our judicious critic. But how great was his surprise, when it was discovered to him, that the said chickens were in pursuit of the hen which had made her escape into the pocket of a soldier!

" Next the sign-post is an honest tar throwing up his hat, crying, ' God bless King George!' Before him is an image of drunken loyalty, who, with his shirt out of his breeches, and bayonet in his hand, vows destruction on the heads of the rebels. A fine figure of a speaking old woman, with a basket upon her head, will upon view tell you what she sells. A humane soldier, perceiving a fellow hard loaded with a barrel of gin upon his back, and stopped by the crowd, with a gimlet bores a hole in the head of the cask, and is kindly easing him of a part of his burthen. Near him is the figure of a fine gentleman in the army. As I suppose the painter designed him without character, I shall therefore only observe, that he is a very pretty fellow; and happily the contemplation of his own dear person guards him from the attempts of the wicked woman on his right hand. Upon the right of this *petit-maitre*, a licentious soldier is rude with a girl, who screams and wreaks her little vengeance upon his face, whilst his comrade is removing some linen that hangs in his way.

"You will pardon the invention of a new term—I shall include the whole King's Head in the word *Cattery*, the principal figure of which is the famous *Mother Douglas*, who, with pious eyes cast up to heaven, prays for the army's success, and the safe return of many of her babes of grace. An officer offers a letter to one of this lady's children, who rejects it; possibly not liking the cause her spark is engaged in, or, what is more probable, his not having paid for her last favour. Above her, a charitable girl is throwing a shilling to a cripple, while another kindly administers a cordial to her companion, as a sure relief against reflection. The rest of the windows are full of the like cattle; and upon the house-top appear three cats, just emblems of the creatures below, but more harmless in their amorous encounter."

King George the Second was told that Hogarth had painted this picture, and wished to have the honour of dedicating to his Majesty the print engraved from it; and a proof-print was accordingly presented for his approbation. The king probably expected to see an allegorical representation of an army of heroes, devoting their lives to the service of their country and their sovereign; we may, therefore, readily conceive his disappointment on viewing their delineation. ' Does the fellow mean to laugh at my guards ? ' exclaimed the indignant monarch to a nobleman in waiting. 'The picture, please your Majesty, must be considered as a burlesque.' 'What! a painter burlesque a soldier? he deserves to be picketed for his insolence.' The print was returned to the artist, who, completely mortified at such a reception of what he properly considered to be his greatest work, immediately altered the inscription, inserting, instead of the King of England, " the King of Prusia (so spelt in the earliest impressions), an encourager of the Arts."

A LARGE SEA-PIECE.

Representing Ships employed in the British Navy, in various positions.

By BROOKING.

A LANDSCAPE.

By GEORGE LAMBERT.

ELIJAH RAISING THE SON OF THE WIDOW OF ZAREPHATH.

" *And he stretched himself upon the child three times, and cried unto the Lord, and said, O Lord my God, I pray thee, let this child's soul come into him again.*

And the Lord heard the voice of Elijah; and the soul of the child came into him again, and he revived."

By LANFRANCO.

PORTRAIT OF HANDEL.
BY SIR GODFREY KNELLER.
Presented by Charles Pott, Esq., a Vice-President.

PORTRAIT IN CRAYONS OF TAYLOR WHITE, ESQ.
(Treasurer of the Hospital from 1746 to 1771),
BY FRANCIS COTES, R.A.

PORTRAIT IN CRAYONS OF GEORGE WHATLEY, ESQ.
(Treasurer of the Hospital from 1779 to 1791),
BY A PERSON UNKNOWN.

PORTRAIT OF CHARLES POTT, ESQ.
(Treasurer from 1839 to 1852, and now a Vice-President)
BY THOMAS PHILLIPS, R.A.
Painted at the request of numerous friends, Governors of the Institution, and presented by them as a testimony of their esteem.

CLEMENT HUE, M.D.
(A Vice-President)
Painted by R. Buckner for several of the Governors, and by them presented to the Hospital as a mark of respect.

THE OFFERING OF THE WISE MEN.
" *And when they were come into the house, they saw the young child with Mary his mother, and fell down, and worshipped him: and when they had opened their treasures, they presented unto him gifts ; gold, and frankincense, and myrrh.*"
BY ANDREW CASALI.

ACTION OFF THE COAST OF FRANCE,

May 13th, 1779.

By LUNY.

The particulars of this Picture are as follows, viz.:—
" *Sir James Wallace, Commander of H. M. Ship Experiment, with the Pallas, Unicorn, Fortunœ, and Cabot, Brigs, attacking the Danœ, Valeur, Recluce, three French Frigates, and a Cutter, in Concale Bay. The Danœ he brought off. The other three being aground, he burnt, amidst a smart fire from a battery of six twelve-pounders, and several cannon from the shore. The battery he silenced in half-an-hour.*"

PORTRAIT OF LORD CHIEF JUSTICE WILMOT,

By DANCE.

BUST OF HANDEL,

By LOUIS FRANCIS ROUBILIAC.

The above bust was taken by the artist from sittings to him by Handel, and is the original work from which the celebrated statue in Vauxhall Gardens and that in Westminster Abbey were made. At the sale of Mr. Barrett, the proprietor of Vauxhall Gardens, the bust was purchased by Mr. Bartleman, and was, for many years, esteemed by him as his greatest treasure. Upon his death, it passed, by sale, into the hands of the trade; and lastly, upon the recommendation of Mr. William Behnes, sculptor, was purchased and presented to the Hospital by Sir Frederick Pollock, Lord Chief Baron of the Exchequer and a Vice-President of the Hospital.

T

Besides this model, there are two busts, namely, one by Behnes of the late Henry Earle, Esq., the eminent Surgeon, who gratuitously gave his professional services to the Children of the Hospital for many years.

The other of the present Morning Preacher, the Rev. J. W. Gleadall, M.A., by S. J. B. Haydon.

PORTRAIT OF GEORGE THE SECOND
(First Patron of the Hospital).
By SHACKLETON.

PORTRAIT OF THE EARL OF DARTMOUTH
(A Vice-President of the Hospital).
By SIR JOSHUA REYNOLDS.

PORTRAIT OF THE EARL OF MACCLESFIELD
(A Vice-President).
By WILSON.

PORTRAIT OF DR. MEAD
(A very active Governor).
By ALLAN RAMSAY.

PORTRAITS OF THEODORE JACOBSEN, ESQ.
(The Architect of the Hospital)
AND JOHN MILNER, ESQ.
(A Governor)
By THOMAS HUDSON.

PORTRAIT OF THOMAS EMMERSON, ESQ.
(A Governor and most liberal Contributor),
BY HIGHMORE.

———

A LARGE SEA-PIECE
(Representing the English Fleet in the Downs).
BY MONAMY.

———

THE CARTOON OF THE MURDER OF THE INNOCENTS.
BY RAFFAEL.

This cartoon came into the possession of the Hospital under the will of Prince Hoare, Esq. The Governors have since lent it to the Trustees of the National Gallery for public exhibition

———

PORTRAIT OF PRINCE HOARE, ESQ.

Presented by his friend and executor, Newbold Kintòn, Esq., a Governor.

———

THE WORTHIES OF ENGLAND.
BY JAMES NORTHCOTES, R.A.

Presented by Newbold Kinton, Esq.

———

PORTRAITS OF SHAKESPERE AND BEN JONSON.

Presented by Frederick Wm. Pott, Esq.

———

HERODIAS WITH THE HEAD OF JOHN THE BAPTIST,

In tapestry, presented by Henry Laver, Esq.

———

There is also a valuable vase of Chelsea porcelain, presented by Dr. Garnier, in 1763.

GOVERNORS AND GUARDIANS

OF THE HOSPITAL, 1858.

Patron.

HER MOST GRACIOUS MAJESTY QUEEN VICTORIA.

President.

HIS ROYAL HIGHNESS THE DUKE OF CAMBRIDGE, K.G.

Vice-Presidents.

THE RIGHT HON. SIR FREDERICK POLLOCK,
Lord Chief Baron of the Exchequer.

CLEMENT HUE, M.D.

JOHN BENJAMIN HEATH, ESQ., F.R.S., F.A.S.

JOHN TRENCHARD TRENCHARD, ESQ.

CHARLES POTT, ESQ.

WILLIAM TOOKE, ESQ., F.R.S.

Treasurer.

GEORGE BURROW GREGORY, ESQ.

1818	John Lavicount Anderdon, Esq.
1819	Henry Alexander, Esq.
1834	Richard Edward Arden, Esq.
1854	John Hungerford Arkwright, Esq.
1813	John Burley, Esq.
1823	Thomas Barlow, Esq.
1835	James Bentley, Esq.
1836	William Burra, Esq.
1842	Patrick Black, M.D.
1844	George Baker, Esq.
1845	Rev. W. P. Baily, M.A.
1847	Beriah Botfield, Esq. M.P.

1847   James B. Bunning, Esq.

1848   Paul Briscoe, Esq.

1818   James Capel, Esq.

1823   James Robert Campbell, Esq.

1839   Benjamin B. Cabbell, Esq.

1847   Robert Cook, Esq.

1851   George Henry Cutler, Esq.

1853   Peter Carthew, Esq.

1855   Daniel Cronin, Esq.

1827   Charles Devon, Esq.

1827   Frederick Devon, Esq.

1828   Bonamy Dobree, Esq.

1828   George Holgate Foster, Esq.

1839   George Forbes, Esq.

1850   Lieut.-General Fair, C.B.

1810   Francis Garrett, Esq.

1827   Charles Gibbes, Esq.

1809   Sir Hungerford Hoskins, Bart.

1833   Benjamin Hawes, Esq.

1841   Robert Amedée Heath, Esq.

1850   Henry Burnley Heath, Esq.

1857   William· Hine, Esq.

1836   William Samuel Jones, Esq.

1852   Saffery William Johnson, Esq.

1836   Newbold Kinton, Esq.

1814   William Nanson Letsom, Esq.

1838   Robert Low, Esq.

1843   Venerable Archdeacon Lawson.

1813   Andrew A. Mieville, Esq.

1853   Rev. Charles Mackenzie, M.A.

1856   Dudley C. Majoribanks, Esq., M.P.

1833   William Nash, Esq.
1843   John Noble, Esq.
1833   John Owen, Esq.
1824   John Pepys, Esq.
1825   Henry Pownall, Esq.
1832   Rev. J. R. Pitman, M.A.
1834   John G. Perry, Esq.
1837   Joseph Compton Pott, Esq.
1839   Arthur Pott, Esq.
1839   William Pott, Esq.
1841   Charles Plumley, Esq.
1845   William Pennington, Esq.
1846   Henry James Perry,. Esq.
1847   Rev. Jeremy Pemberton, M.A.
1856   John Tidd Pratt, Esq.
1810   Daniel Rowland, Esq.
1843   Henry S. Roots, M.D.
1824   John Hugh Smyth, Esq.
1835   Henry F. Stephenson, Esq.
1837   Daniel Sutton, Esq.
1838   John Salt, Esq.
1838   John Spurgin, M.D.
1841   William Salt, Esq.
1852   Rev. Edward Scobell, M.A.
1854   George John Steer, Esq.
1857   Thomas Mitchell Shadwell, Esq.
1810   Claude G. Thornton, Esq.
1839   William James Thompson, Esq.
1839   James Thomas Trimmer, Esq.
1842   Alexander Tweedie, M.D.
1836   George Wigg, Esq.

1837   Samuel Wheeler, Esq.
1839   Stephen P. White, Esq.
1841   William Foster White, Esq.
1842   Edward Weyman Wadeson, Esq.
1845   Rev. Alfred Williams, M.A.
1847   Thomas Wormald, Esq.
1851   John Francis White, Esq.
1812   John Adolphus Young, Esq.

The Members of Her Majesty's Most Honourable Privy Council, for the time being, are also Governors and Guardians of the Hospital by the Charter of Incorporation.

THE END.

Printed by W. & H. S. Warr, 63, High Holborn, and 3, Red Lion Passage,

www.ingramcontent.com/pod-product-compliance
Ingram Content Group UK Ltd.
Pitfield, Milton Keynes, MK11 3LW, UK
UKHW030902150625
459647UK00021B/2665